ATMOSPHERE

ATMOSPHERE

THE SEVEN ELEMENTS OF GREAT DESIGN

James Michael Howard

WRITTEN WITH ANDREW SESSA

FOREWORD BY NEWELL TURNER

ABRAMS, NEW YORK

This book is most affectionately dedicated to my wife, Phoebe,
without whose encouragement, love, support,
good humor, and talent it simply wouldn't have been possible.
(Life wouldn't be much fun without her, either.)

FOREWORD

While it's a given that the places we call home should provide shelter, there is more to creating truly great rooms than shopping for the essentials and playing with the decorative elements.

I remember the first time I walked into an apartment designed by Jim Howard. There were details everywhere that caught my attention: exquisite architectural features, mesmerizing colors, and the touch of luxurious fabrics on the upholstery, to name just a few. But the real impression those rooms made on me was much deeper. They simply felt wonderful to be in, and you never forget rooms with that kind of subliminal appeal.

Interior designers play many practical roles and employ an astonishing array of skills in the practice of their craft. But the most talented among them are actually artists—if not downright alchemists—able to transform the blank canvas of four walls, a floor, and a ceiling into something I've come to think of as "poetry in space."

When a room has good bones to start, decoration doesn't have to do much heavy lifting. Most spaces don't have such wonderful architectural bones, however, and in those instances it takes a designer as skilled as Jim to transform the ordinary into the extraordinary. His interiors are so appropriate, and so beautiful, you really can't imagine that before he worked his indelible magic the spaces could have possibly been sad or lacking in polish.

You can feel the sense of atmosphere in the rooms Jim creates, something that may be more important these days than ever before. Our homes should be our sanctuaries in every sense of the word, and, when imagined by the right discriminating, sophisticated eye, their designs can have the ability to nurture and elevate life through the substance of beauty. Jim Howard has just such an eye; he is a master at making rooms magically come alive.

Newell Turner
Editorial Director, Hearst Design Group
ELLE Decor, House Beautiful, and *Veranda*

INTRODUCTION

Atmosphere is the magic that an entire residence can have when it is beautifully designed—the complex murmur of mood and undercurrent of refinement in a lovely setting. It embodies the power a space has to capture your attention and please your senses, embracing you and making your eyes dance around your surroundings. It is the "wow factor."

But even as atmosphere can excite and animate, it can also soothe and calm. And that's of equal importance, because it offers an overall feeling of well-being, ease, and contentment. Spaces with atmosphere are both comfortable and comforting.

To recall an instance when you experienced a place like this, think of a building or an interior that triggered a seemingly contradictory combination of stimulation and relaxation. For me, it's when I first saw Mario Buatta's famed blue-and-white bedroom at New York's Kips Bay Decorator Show House, where the dynamic, curtained, and fringed canopy bed in the middle of the space almost grazed the ceiling. Thanks to its signature butter-yellow color and the way it plays with baroque scale, classical proportions, and natural light, the late British decorator Nancy Lancaster's famed drawing room behind the Colefax & Fowler shop on London's Brook Street also all but blew me away when I had the chance to see it. And atmosphere isn't just reserved for traditional design or for residences. The overall effect of Frank Gehry's titanium-clad Walt Disney Concert Hall—and the pleasure people take from visiting it—comes from the entirely contemporary feats of architectural acrobatics achieved by its gentle curves, both inside and out.

Each of these places makes manifest a supreme sense of atmosphere. Not only does their aesthetic beauty resonate with us but also their consistency, authenticity, relevancy, and, above all, their humanity. They are correctly designed, to be sure, but also awesome and awe-inspiring.

People often imagine that interior designers and decorators simply create and decorate spaces—putting a wall here, hanging curtains there, selecting a light fixture for the ceiling, a color for the wall. But to think like that is to miss the larger picture. The mission of designers such as myself goes much deeper, and our goals are much loftier.

Only by carefully considering and thoughtfully combining the seven elements of great design—style, scale and proportion, rhythm, light, color, texture, and sound—will interiors have atmosphere. Their balance is the secret to creating rooms and residences that impress and inspire.

I became a designer because I had a passion for helping my clients make homes that achieve a profound sense of atmosphere, and I've committed my career to that goal.

It was a childhood visit to the historic Mediterranean revival Miami mansion-turned-museum Vizcaya that first gave me an appreciation of atmosphere, and, as I look back on it, it's also probably what ignited my passion for design and drove me to the profession in the first place. I was about fourteen at the time, growing up in Florida, and my parents made sure I was exposed to wonders like this—locations and experiences that would expand my horizons and inspire my future. And it worked.

The architecture and decoration of Vizcaya didn't just impress me, however; they moved me emotionally, making a profound sentimental impact on my young self that was unlike any other I'd previously experienced. I remember thinking at the time, *One day, I wouldn't mind doing something like this, creating a place with such aesthetic importance and emotional power.*

Prior to that Vizcaya visit, I never really dreamed of being a designer. Where I was raised, in the years that I was coming of age, it didn't quite seem like a career possibility. In high school, I took a job driving the delivery truck for a local furniture store after class and on Saturdays. Later, as graduation approached, I knew I wanted to get myself to New York City, and I thought of the furniture business as something that could take me there.

I had a vague idea of a design college in Manhattan called Parsons. On something of a whim, I applied. The school accepted me, and to this day, I consider my studies there as some of the greatest years and one of the most influential forces of my life. I discovered, and then significantly deepened, my passion for design at Parsons, and I became smitten with the idea of creating lasting, important houses. I am still following that dream.

Ultimately, I learned to be a designer by designing, by making mistakes, and by making progress. I would draw and sketch and create rooms over and over and over, improving the details, honing my craft, studying the end product, learning what to do, and, just as importantly, what not to do.

I've written this book to convey what I've learned about crafting atmosphere at home, wherever that home may be, whatever aesthetic it might have. Doing so isn't a matter of rules or formulas, but there is a science to it as much as an art. And while it requires knowledge, passionate research, and travel, it also benefits from a willingness to think inventively, creatively, and in multiple dimensions. As much fun as creating atmosphere can be, it's also hard work, and there are no easy solutions, no shortcuts—no good ones, anyway.

As I discovered in my earliest days at Parsons—in a class taught by Allen Tate, a fellow Southerner who headed the school's department of environmental design—we create atmosphere by carefully considering, and then just as carefully managing and balancing, *the seven elements of great design*. These elements are *style, scale and proportion, rhythm, light, color, texture*, and *sound*. Only when each element is fully and thoughtfully considered, not just on its own but also in relation to all the others, will spaces provide an immersive, experiential sense of atmosphere.

In these pages, I'll define and describe these seven elements, first taking a look at each on its own—both in the abstract and in actual rooms—and then all together, across several homes I've designed. Doing so will illustrate how the elements work together to create atmosphere.

When a space has atmosphere, it has a message, and it can tell an almost indescribably emotional story. That message, that story, is born out of the homeowners' interests, passions, history, and collections, spun and edited by a passionate and experienced interior designer. A good design professional expertly uses the seven elements to weave together a story that draws people in and makes them want to stay, lingering and luxuriating in the atmosphere of a home.

The seven elements persist because they are the building blocks of atmosphere. They remind us of what's of paramount importance when creating a scheme for a space, and they help us find good solutions with every choice and decision that we make in any given interior—and there are hundreds of them.

With this book, I want to share what I have learned about atmosphere, from a core theoretical understanding of the seven elements of good design to their real-life application at home. These elements provide me and my studio with an underlying structure for our projects: They let our designs emerge in a disciplined way, and with controls. But they also let our creativity soar and our aesthetic acumen shine. An ability to expertly handle these intangible elements—as much as our skill in making specific choices for cabinets, fabrics, light fixtures, and other fittings and furnishings—is our greatest asset. The seven elements allow us to lead our projects, large or small, rather than letting the projects lead us.

The elements have guided, and continue to guide, my designs down a remarkable path. They are what I use every day to create spaces with the greatest sense of atmosphere possible—warm, welcoming, and downright magical rooms and residences that people love to call home.

PART I

THE SEVEN ELEMENTS
OF GREAT DESIGN

The most effective way for me to plan a house is to develop its design holistically, not as a series of individual choices about furnishings, objects, and colors, but as the pursuit of something more profound and emotional. That "something" is atmosphere—the single note in a space that is greater than the sum of its parts. The seven elements of great design allow me to approach an interior in an organized and disciplined manner, but, even more importantly, they help me imaginatively create atmosphere.

While there are many fundamental design principles I subscribe to, I embrace these seven elements above all. Every decision I make for an interior has consequences, so each requires rationale and thoughtfulness about how today's decisions will affect tomorrow's outcome. Considering each of these elements, both separately and together, ensures continuity and cohesion.

To create a home that is indeed atmospheric, one must dig a little deeper and explore the bigger picture with increased care. When presented with a new design idea, one must take time to think, pondering how it will fit into the seven elements and help create atmosphere. The elements allow the designer to stay focused and keenly aware of what will make a beautiful interior, one in which life can unfold in the most remarkable of ways.

In the seven chapters of this section, I'll define each of the elements, starting with style and ending with sound—the same order I use when designing. I'll explain how I think about and use that element and then show how I've deployed it in a variety of compelling and carefully completed homes.

I

STYLE

The first of the seven elements is style. It is no more important than the six others, but it *is* the starting point, determining the direction and character of an entire scheme.

"Style" in this case doesn't refer to the vague idea of a space's having élan—that is, of its being "chic" or "stylish" or "fashionable." And it's not about *my* style, or even necessarily just about the personal style of a house's residents. Rather, it's about the prevailing look suggested by a number of factors, from the homeowners' preferences to the aesthetic of a building's exterior and its surroundings. Are we in Palm Beach, where the vernacular architecture is Spanish Colonial, or in Rhode Island or the Hamptons, where it's the shingle style? Do we want the interior to have a traditional attitude or a modern or contemporary one? More specifically, will it be American mid-century modern, say, or country French, or Art Deco?

Over the years, I've learned that the most successful way to design is to consider a specific style and then consistently maintain its unique parameters. Rules give structure and discipline, and this specificity helps create order and integrity that ultimately leads to a sense of atmosphere.

This is not to say that we must be slaves to the constraints of a single aesthetic. We're not designing period rooms in a museum here. I often create houses in a classically inspired, nineteenth- or twentieth-century idiom but include a more modern chef's kitchen with an amply sized adjoining family room. It has always served me well, however, to know exactly what a style's guidelines are and to work in close relation to them.

This might mean an adherence to the edited-down rooms and neutral color palettes of modernism, or it could be the heavily molded interiors, fanciful curtains, and eighteenth- and nineteenth-century European furniture of traditional houses.

Though it contains objects from around the world—a French mantel, for example, and wooden bowls from Afghanistan—the design direction of this living room is one of relaxed, traditionally inspired American country-house comfort. It's the mood telegraphed here by the slipcovered upholstery, the plank-top cocktail table, and the grass rug.

Filled with a lovely mix of Belgian, French, and Italian furnishings, this house was imagined as Continental European in style, reflecting the homeowners' roots. They envisioned living in spaces of restrained beauty, whose modern sensibility would be visually calming. In keeping with that goal, this room is chaste and spare, with plaster walls, minimal moldings, antiqued oak floors, and contemporary paintings.

We often think of stylistic choices in terms of casual or formal, rustic or refined. A casual room might give you the feeling of a warm embrace. Its organic materials and more raw finishes make it feel worn in, collected, even shabby, but in a charming way. A formal room has more elevated appeal, captivating you with its pairing of complementary objects, refined furnishings, and expensive materials that are sophisticated and precious—think carved furniture, boiserie, parquetry floors, and precious marble elements.

Some genres are inherently more or less formal. The shingle style, which got its start around the turn of the twentieth century in seaside towns in the Northeast, tends toward the informal and relaxed. With its asymmetrical, rambling, and slightly quirky look, it's beautiful but not exactly elegant. The atmosphere created by the Colonial American neoclassical federal style, in contrast—seen at the White House and in many Philadelphia townhouses—is one of formality. It's light in feeling, with smooth surfaces, precisely carved detailing in moldings and furniture, and the use of more rarified materials and methods.

A designer's job is to help homeowners determine which style is right for them and their house and, just as important, to help them understand why. To do so, we must listen to what the homeowners are saying about their vision for their project, without necessarily asking them to describe their aesthetic. Sometimes nothing needs to be said at all; designers can tell what clients like and don't like by what's already in their homes, and by their reactions to suggestions and to images they are shown.

Once you've established the style for a project, you don't want to swerve far from its prescribed path, even if you see something new that you absolutely love in a magazine or maybe in a friend's home. Consistency is key when it comes to overall style. It is essential to remain true to an aesthetic intention, and to continue on the fairly straight and the relatively narrow with it. Doing so will best serve the creation of atmosphere.

A collection of nineteenth-century architectural engravings from Italy proved just the thing to adorn the staircase of this Italian-style villa. Found hidden away in a box under a bed, they were a stunning discovery. Setting them in matching frames keeps the focus on the images themselves, which are arranged in a freeform collage accented by a pair of Venetian sconces. The ensemble plays like a lovely melody up the dynamic steps.

The best quality
designs of any
classical period
will almost always
mix and mingle
with great élan.

Designed in a strictly traditional idiom, my own
Atlanta apartment has rooms that are classic in
style and rich with detail. Here, in the living room,
painted raised panels adorned with egg and dart
carving and dentil and acanthus leaf tip moldings
cover the walls. Classical furnishings, including a
George II mirror, finish the scheme.

Modern and contemporary art need not be used exclusively with twentieth- and twenty-first century architecture and design. Such pieces work well even in largely traditional interiors, as can be seen above, in the art hung amid damasks over a cabriole-leg table, and opposite, in the pale painting set against similarly hued raised paneling, overlooking an oval table surrounded by Queen Anne–style chairs.

Even with its Shaker-fronted cabinetry, this kitchen
has a modern sensibility. Stripped of all things
decorative, the space has no cornice, architrave, or other
ornamental design elements. Rather, the story
is one of restraint and simplicity of style. The finishes—
including plaster walls and ceilings as smooth to the
touch as porcelain—look completely pure. This discipline
makes the room appear as sublimely appropriate now as
it would have in the past. It is timeless.

2

SCALE & PROPORTION

In design and architecture, "scale" refers to the size of one object in relation to another, with the second object usually being the human form, while "proportion" is the relative size of the parts of an object to the entire thing.

Think of it this way: "Scale" is the size of a room, how big or small it is compared to people; "proportion" is the boldness or heft (or lack thereof) of the decoration in the space. This element must also be considered for every aspect of a room—the proportion of the print on a fabric to the scale of the armchair it covers, say, or the relationship between the height of a cabinet and the size of its drawers.

Scale and proportion help guide all the choices that must be made in a space, facilitating decisions about everything from moldings to door heights, sofas to lighting. As with style, they must be handled consistently to be used successfully. This creates harmony between the size of a room and of what goes into it.

Compare early-eighteenth-century French Régence furniture, for example, which has robust and grand proportions, to late-eighteenth-century English Robert Adam furnishings, which are delicate and slight. Neither is objectively *better* than the other, but the decision of which to choose requires consideration of the differences between the scale of a room and the proportion of its decoration: Régence is more often appropriate in a large room; Adam in a small one.

Scale and proportion don't necessarily have to remain unchanged across a residence. While you wouldn't want to deploy the weight of Régence in the living area and the lightness of Adam in an adjacent dining room, or mix the two in one space, you can play with scale and proportion from room to room. The Italians perhaps understood this best, taking the grandeur of the façade of a hilltop villa and then shrinking both scale and proportion in the entryway and adjacent

In a grandly scaled foyer—featuring a staircase nearly five feet wide and a ceiling height of more than twenty-four feet—a hanging cobalt-blue glass lantern, black metal balustrade, and tea-paper ceiling have enough substance to remain in proportion with the large room, even as the lightness of their design and materials prevents the space from being weighted down by its overall size.

passages, only to expand them again in a grand hall or loggia. The two change in concert with each other to ensure that the relationship between them remains consistent from room to room, even as the size of the spaces may change: more delicate details and furnishings in smaller spaces, weightier decor in larger ones.

No matter how large a house is, many homeowners these days generally prefer to occupy rooms that have intimacy. We may like to visit grand European house museums like England's Blenheim Palace or France's Malmaison, but we don't necessarily want to live in their gigantic rooms. When we sit down at home, we prefer to be close to our spouse, our family, our friends. We want to be near them to have a conversation.

This is not to say that houses today can't have any rooms of significant size. We want to accommodate multigenerational family get-togethers and the occasional big party, as well as several different purposes all in a single open-plan area. People want great rooms for entertaining and master suites with sitting areas, fireplaces, dressing rooms, and home offices. But then we discover we don't entertain as often as we expected, and couples all but lose each other within their oversize boudoirs.

The trick to making even the biggest of rooms feel human-scaled is to keep their decoration in proportion with their overall dimensions. This allows them to seem smaller than they actually are and cozier than they might otherwise be. Doing so might mean bringing ceiling heights slightly lower, or, in a room with very high ceilings, using tall wainscoting and heavier crown moldings to make the space appear shorter, breaking down its scale. Usually, selecting larger furniture whose proportions are in accord with the size of a room, as well as bolder art, will ensure the most pleasing of schemes. Think of a robust four-poster bed in a spacious guest room, for example. You could also create several arrangements of smaller furniture within one space. That's a strategy I'll frequently deploy in great rooms that have living, dining, entertaining, and kitchen areas, and master suites that incorporate space for sleeping, sitting by a fireplace, watching TV, and working. Rooms like this can feel at once expansive *and* intimate—and, as a result, full of atmosphere.

OPPOSITE: This two-story, vaulted living room demanded decor that would feel proportionate to its immense size. To that end, a pair of custom six-foot-tall Alberto Giacometti–style iron lanterns hang between massive oak timber trusses, and a monumental Tudor-style mantel surrounds a firebox that's nearly five feet by five feet. PREVIOUS PAGES: Similar strategies were deployed in this space, with the clean lines of accents and accessories complementing the proportions of the chimneypiece and beams.

A mammoth seventeenth-century-style French stone mantel, with an enormous trumeau, provides an anchor and focal point for this dining room. The Gothic vitrines flanking it broaden the profound proportions across the room. Emphasizing the massive mantle and vitrines are a table and chairs that feel lighter, the better to recede. When everything in a room has the same weight or power, the room's atmosphere can suffer.

Lowering the color contrast in large spaces helps them feel more intimate. Fabrics can have a similar effect, especially when they are gathered and have faint, faded patterns.

A large, dramatic canopy bed is just the thing to ensure that a very tall or otherwise large bedroom still offers coziness. I designed this nearly ten-foot-tall bed, with an antiqued gilded cornice that provides a lovely juxtaposition to the steel posts. It rests beautifully under a vaulted Italianate ceiling whose subtle leaf pattern is over-painted with soft glazes.

3

RHYTHM

Rhythm is the creation of harmony and balance in a room or across a residence. It promotes a sense of order, which, in turn, leads to atmosphere. A desire for rhythm helps determine the placement of all furnishings and details in every space I design. It guides me to evenly distribute the weight of a room's floor plan, wall elevations, and furniture arrangements to craft a scheme that's ordered and organized. Such order and organization don't require symmetry to be cohesive and logical, however. Rhythm allows for an asymmetrical symmetry that keeps things interesting in a room, the same way syncopation might in a piece of music.

Rhythm brings beauty and comfort to spaces suffering from poor planning or lackluster architecture. In that way, it's like a decorating Band-Aid. It helps us create equilibrium amid chaos. In a room with oddly positioned windows, an off-center fireplace, or a single door on one end of a focal wall, for example, you might deploy art, furniture, color, and other architectural details to create a rhythmic arrangement that offsets the imbalance. Or, in a room with tall, narrow windows whose scale and proportion are a bit funky, you could design full, voluminous curtains that would hang from a rod extending past the edges of each window. That would correct the proportion and restore the right rhythm.

I often talk about rhythm in relation to the rule of advancing and receding. This rule is about finding a rhythmic balance between elements that should stand out and those that should hang back in a space. If you walk into a room and everything in it is of equal importance, you don't know where to look, and the overall sense of atmosphere suffers. Designers can control the viewer's eye and so must consider what they want people to see when they first walk into a room. We get to pick and create the focal point, developing an arrangement—or two—that causes that point to advance and the rest to recede.

A room with rhythm is as wonderful as any good symphony. It engenders simultaneous feelings of serenity and energy that define spaces with great atmosphere.

Thinking about rhythm in a space helps establish equilibrium without relying on absolute symmetry. Here, the shelving niche on the right mirrors the cased archway on the left, while the use of two different chairs on either side of the fireplace adds a dose of syncopation. Though slightly asymmetrical, the design is still balanced.

PREVIOUS PAGES: Strict symmetry, while beautiful, will sometimes be a little too formal. An amorphic sculpture—which almost seems to be the inspiration for the painting—placed to one side of the console loosens this space up a bit, inserting a rhythmic twist. THIS PAGE: In a comfortable, casual country house, try to avoid using matching pairs of anything. Selecting two different but in some way complementary chairs, lamps, or tables relaxes the rhythm of a room, resulting in a more collected-looking appearance and laid-back atmosphere.

4

LIGHT

As the ultimate mood-maker, light is a primary ingredient of atmosphere. Whether natural, electric, or provided by candles, it can be a room's—and a designer's—best friend.

In the most obvious sense, light is an important design element because it allows a space to be seen, appreciated, and enjoyed. But it offers much more than just literal illumination and brightness. Light can make a room feel warm and affable, or it can keep things reserved. It will bring your awareness to certain objects and spaces, letting them advance as focal points, while casting others into darkness, making them recede. Light creates highlights and shadows, shape and substance, and, very often, drama and romance. It can provide a room with a sense of poetry.

We must look at light in regard to more prosaic considerations, too. Practically speaking, you need strong, clear task lighting near a favorite reading chair, or in a home office or kitchen, so the work at hand can be completed. You want brightness in a bathroom or dressing room for putting on makeup or selecting clothes, but dining and living rooms sometimes call for softer illumination.

There are also negative consequences of light that you must control—glare from sun coming through a naked window or bouncing off reflective surfaces, or unintentional shadows thrown by an overhead fixture. All this must be contemplated as you think about this element and how to use it to create atmosphere.

A successful design scheme will provide the right light for a house at every hour. As the sun moves across the sky throughout the day, it causes our perception of color and texture to change. Using dimmers can mitigate this, but it's also necessary to think about how every room in a house will be used from morning to night and the direction the sun comes from at various points. Then, you can place sconces, pendants, table and floor lamps, curtains, shades, and other window treatments.

Too often, we drape, shade, or otherwise cover every window with some costly, theatrical treatment. Remember, light is your friend. If a window is super-sized and beautiful, use it, unadorned, to allow a room to come alive.

Reflected light can be just as important—and useful—as direct light. **PAGE 46:** The simple Continental-style iron mirror hangs at a right angle to multiple French doors, which helps send the sun around the room. **PAGE 47:** A tea-paper ceiling softly throws light from the clerestory window around this stair landing and down into the foyer below. **THIS PAGE:** In a kitchen, all-encompassing ambient light offers warmth, and decorative lamps add charm, but task lighting is an absolute necessity when wielding a sharp knife or working over a hot flame. Using multiple sources—including pendants, under-cabinet lighting, and recessed fixtures that can be focused on the workspace, countertops, and appliances—provides various options for different needs or scenes.

Natural light is a key ingredient in the most pleasing of rooms. Spaces that enjoy direct sunshine have atmospheres of warmth and joy.

Sun bathes this two-story drawing room from high to low, back to front, side to side. The window walls—whose bright light can be managed with sheer patterned curtains—are twenty-one feet wide, while the clerestory washes the sun down and across the walls, beams, and ceiling. Sitting here feels like being in a solarium.

Understanding light's impact will help you harness its usefulness. The best houses have natural light on at least two sides. Ideally, the sun hits one side from the south. This gives the most direct natural light for the longest time, leading to a brighter, warmer, happier atmosphere. When in the room-planning stages of a design project, you should use south-facing spaces as those where you will spend the most daylight time—the kitchen, the breakfast room, and the family room, for example.

Southern is not the only exposure of value, however. East-facing spaces make wonderful bedrooms and breakfast areas, capturing morning sun. Looking west from a dining table provides sunset views. Rooms with northern exposure, meanwhile, will glow quietly—making them perfect bedrooms for those who are decidedly *not* morning people.

When it comes to electric lighting, the possibilities are enticingly endless, comprising myriad selections of fixtures (chandeliers, pendants, sconces, recessed, track, table and floor lamps) and light types (incandescent, halogen, fluorescent, LED), plus shade materials (silk, parchment, linen, metal) and shapes (square, cylindrical, triangular). Two key factors for figuring out which you'll want for any given space are the direction a room's windows face and the room's function. Then, think about the furniture plan and illumination it requires, as well as the materials you've used and how they might best be lit.

Sconces illuminate your face in a bathroom and light your living room in places where table lamps can't go, while recessed fixtures with incandescent bulbs provide the best task lighting and overall illumination in a kitchen. Bedrooms benefit from the flexibility of chandeliers and table and floor lamps; romantic and dreamy, these fixtures can tell a story. Chandeliers can even create a candlelight effect, especially when dimmed; their multiple bulbs and reflective elements cause light to dance around, throwing illumination everywhere, usually in small doses. Recessed lighting around the edges of a room reflects light off walls, making them appear to recede. This causes a room to look larger. Placing table lamps in front of hanging mirrors or picture lights above glass-covered artworks results in a sparkling look that's ideal in entertaining spaces. It can be glitzy, warm, and dramatic.

Controlling what we see and how we see it is crucial to creating atmosphere. A good lighting scheme will be layered and developed in concert with a furniture plan to bring attention to the most beautiful aspects of a room.

We wake up with the sun and go to bed when it leaves us. Even for those late sleepers among us, there is often nothing more delightful than its warmth on our face, or the way it throws shadows throughout the day, highlighting the rich and soft textures that are ideal in a bedroom.

ABOVE: In this sun-filled bedroom, tactile fabrics, including chenille and linen, take advantage of the abundant natural light, which enhances our perception of the textures. OPPOSITE: This sleeping chamber greets the day through a majestic, double-height arched window. Since natural light can wash out saturated colors, a pale palette of light blues, ochres, and neutrals proves just right.

5

COLOR

When you first walk into a room, you may not notice its sense of scale or light right away, but, chances are, you'll immediately find yourself moved by its color palette. The colors might energize you, make you feel calm and relaxed, or intrigued by their powerful hold on you. Color resonates differently with each of us, but it affects us all in one way or another, and that's why it is such an important ingredient in atmosphere.

Although it's only one element among the seven elements of great design, color is actually made up of three components: hue, intensity, and chroma. Each serves atmosphere differently, so the entire trio should be considered together. And remember: Color extends far beyond paint choices; it's also a consideration for textiles, carpets, metal, wood, marble, glass, and artwork.

Let's start with hue. It's the component we most often think of as the "color" itself—red, blue, green, chartreuse, periwinkle, etc. Those used in an interior are usually based on the personal preferences of a homeowner. Within any hue are nuances that make the color cooler or warmer. This is especially easy to see in neutrals, where a beige might have a warm undertone of yellow, or a gray might have a cool hint of blue. But it's not just neutrals: A lavender will feel warmer when it has more red than blue, and a green cooler with more blue than yellow.

The next component is intensity, which many design professionals call "value." It refers to a color's level of pigment saturation. Colors that are saturated with pigment are said to have a lot of intensity; those with less pigment have lower saturation and, therefore, less intensity. Take the hue orange: A version with high intensity would be deep, dark terra-cotta; pale peach, however, has low intensity. Intense colors lend a room a bold or moody atmosphere. Those with

The neutral tones used everywhere else in this room strengthen the effect of the particular shades of blue in the painting hung over the oak cabinet.

less saturation provide a subtler, more serene air. Adding white to a color will make it less intense, as will adding its complementary hue—red grays out green, for example, and orange does the same to blue. The complement acts as a so-called "kill color," knocking down the intensity.

The final component is chroma. Technically, chroma is a color's light reflectance value (LRV), but you can think of it as brightness. It doesn't exactly refer to luster or shininess, but rather to how much light a color absorbs or reflects—its almost luminescent quality. LRV is measured on a scale from zero to a hundred: True black has an LRV of zero, because it absorbs all light; pure white has an LRV of one hundred, reflecting any light shone on it. High LRV colors can do especially well in rooms without a lot of natural light, but in a room with tons of sun, they might be overwhelming.

When establishing a project's palette, you must consider all three of color's components, but it's best to first decide on a warm or cool atmosphere. That's because colors with different temperatures won't always work together. A great tool for highlighting the coolness or warmth of a palette, however, is to insert one accent color that's just the opposite—a flash of hot chrome yellow amid an otherwise cool, deep eggplant, say.

Once you've settled on cool or warm, you can pull specific hues from a favorite rug, painting, or textile you'll feature in the space. You already know you find its color combination appealing, so you can use it as a starting point. If you don't have something to work from, try developing a scheme by varying the intensity of a single favorite hue, combining colors with different levels of saturation. This is a trick pulled from nature: If you look at an apple, you'll notice there are dozens of shades of red on the skin; if you had only half of them, you'd lose something. The same is true of the greens of a zucchini, the creamy ivories on a white-sand beach, and the golden beiges in a block of limestone. All those slightly different colors, working in concert with each other, make these things beautiful—and they'll make your room beautifully atmospheric.

Brown is never just brown. Every color, whether light or dark, will have warm undertones of red, orange, or yellow, or cooler ones of blue, green, or purple. Here, a deep brown offers a refined, earthy richness that sets off the nineteenth-century engravings and faded-salmon patina of a bureau bookcase.

A wonderful way to develop your palette is to stretch a single hue along the tonal spectrum from darkest to lightest, most saturated to least saturated. Doing so creates colors that work wonderfully together.

White has proven to be perennially popular in kitchens for good reason: It creates an atmosphere that feels clean, and it makes everything around it look great, showing off the true, rich colors of produce and plates of lovingly presented food. Here, the light blue of the lacquered ceiling reflects the sky, as does the upholstery on the stools, which is a more intense version of the hue used above.

6

TEXTURE

This element hardly needs definition: Texture is the way something feels to you when you touch it, the roughness or smoothness against your skin. But in relation to interior design, texture also refers to how different materials *look*: the shine of a lacquered ceiling, the matte softness of a thick piled carpet, the fine weave of linen on a wall.

These tactile and visual qualities have significance both when you're selecting an individual item—a piece of furniture, a length of fabric, a type of art—and when you're thinking about an entire room, as well as a complete residence. A home achieves an overall sense of texture through the combination of complementary and contrasting surface treatments applied to each design component. The careful mix of sumptuous textures adds to the delight and enjoyment of a space, contributing to its atmosphere.

Successfully mixing and juxtaposing different finishes doesn't mean using whatever tactile materials happen to appeal to you, however. Remember: The "art of the mix" is referred to as an "art" for a reason. Selecting and combining the right materials and finishes requires a careful eye and plenty of consideration. There's no hard-and-fast scientific rule for how to do it, but it helps to contemplate every decision, thinking long and hard about each, and then adhering to what you know *will* work, rather than what you hope *might* work.

Everything has texture, so each feature of a room will have its own tactile qualities. Properly layering them requires an awareness of all the surfaces and materials to be used—and the differences between them. Spaces with too many textures lack cohesion and beauty. A house of a thousand flung-together finishes has a similarly confusing effect as one that tries to recklessly mix together several styles.

To guarantee success, make sure to have some degree of textural contrast, sometimes more, sometimes less. A bit of contrast helps emphasize every design

The various tactile components of a room will be appreciated visually as well as physically. Here, the contrast between the two heathered tones in the rug creates an appearance of texture that's as important as the actual roughness and smoothness of the various woods, metals, stones, and textiles used elsewhere in the space.

The right mix of textures can generate a welcoming, embracing atmosphere—just what you want in a foyer. In this entry, the faux-graining on the paneled walls and the natural edges and weathered surface of the antique French limestone floor telegraph warmth and comfort, as does the pair of commodious low cabinets.

component, highlighting the differences between and unique qualities of each. Without one, you don't understand the other. In some settings, you want smooth against rough—highly textured stone objects on a glass surface, say, or a shiny antiqued mirror rather than a heavily painted piece of art on a stucco wall. Other times, similarly treated but still different surfaces will work best together: Smooth modern objects on a rough-hewn country pine table will not be as lovely as they would be on a polished marble-topped console. A chenille pillow won't look right on a silk velvet sofa, even in the perfect color; try something smoother and more luxurious. The look and feel of antique French limestone floors and modern lacquered walls are great—just not together. Each material must complement and enhance the other. The goal is to create a mix, not a mash.

Varying textures becomes especially vital when you're working with a neutral or monochromatic color palette. In these sorts of schemes, the interest provided by texture replaces that of hue. The rooms still have plenty going on, a wealth of architectural information, and myriad decorative details to make up for the fact that there's not a strong use of color. Instead, texture becomes the central sensory element.

Texture also directly relates to the element of rhythm. Deploying different ones helps create a sense of balance and order, as well as syncopation, around a room, and changing textures from room to room does the same across an entire house. If one space has plain walls and floors, or an otherwise relatively simple textural palette, then the next room could have richly grained wood paneling or wainscoting or antique stone or brick floors. You change the textural treatment to make the scheme more interesting.

The right combinations and layers of texture make a house look and feel comfortable and full of character—and that helps a home's residents and guests feel relaxed and cozy. Our sensory perception of splendid textures triggers a fundamental part of our brains, one that can stimulate and excite us, or calm and soothe us. It's a subconscious, intuitive response, not unlike our appreciation of atmosphere itself.

The luxurious linen covering a Jean-Michel Frank–style sofa plays off the armchairs' smooth leather. Under the seating vignette, the Nepalese wool carpet has been naturally dyed and then aged in some places to give it a marvelous timeworn feeling. You can never go wrong with organic materials like these: They have innate soul and character.

Textured walls elevate the aesthetic and enhance the coziness of this basement-level gathering area. A blend of sand and joint compound was troweled on in a grid, then painted over in shades of sepia and pale umber.

Decorative painting shouldn't always be too studied or realistic—it may not even require an artist. Try using colors from a room's palette as transparent washes, blending them together. **ABOVE:** Panels of lime-washed white-oak plywood fit together in a checkerboard of perpendicular grains. **OPPOSITE:** Several coats of diluted paint on paneling provide the perfect backdrop for the similarly layered Jim Dine heart painting.

Kitchens are often defined by their cabinet style, but here a desire for a rustic look required material depth and variety. While most counters are marble, the top of this island is distressed wood, and the raised-panel design changes from one set of cabinets to the next, so they seem more like furniture from different makers that was collected over time. A tactile dragged finish unifies it all.

As the place in a home where people most fully let down their guards, a bedroom benefits from sumptuous textiles and soft natural fibers. They help you completely relax. Here, handmade floral-patterned paper on the walls, a wool-and-silk carpet, and lots of nubby fabrics, including the Brazilian lamb's wool used for the pillows, envelop the space in an organic way.

7

SOUND

We all love lively conversation over supper in a friend's dining room, but sometimes you find the table is so wide and the unadorned walls so echoing that it's impossible to hear anything anyone is saying, and you have to practically shout to be understood. Or maybe you've sat chatting in a formal living room where the serene mood is interrupted every time a garage door opens or closes. Fewer of us, however, may have had another kind of experience of sound at home: Drinking coffee in a breakfast room from which you can enjoy a spouse's piano-playing as it wafts in from the den, or reading in a family room where you can hear the laughter of children in the yard.

Aural considerations like these are undoubtedly the most overlooked of the elements of great design. But while sound may be listed as the last of the seven elements, it certainly isn't the least. An awareness of it, an understanding of its effects, and a strategy for how to control it are as important as the choices you make regarding style, rhythm, and color. And sound must be taken into consideration early in the design process to prevent costly, and sometimes irreversible, mistakes.

We usually only note the effects of sound on atmosphere if they're negative, but they can make positive contributions, too. We may want voices to travel across a great room, for example, so that people cooking in the kitchen area can talk to others on the sofa. Or a living room might have several conversation zones, each with enough fabric and upholstery to dampen voices, so those close by can speak at normal volume while others elsewhere in the space do the same—all without the noise level becoming a cacophony of discordant sounds. At a beach house, you want to hear the surf breaking as you drift off to sleep; and in a woodland country home, crickets chirping and wind rustling. I take all of these possibilities into account when designing interiors.

Few design features can turn a room into a restful retreat quite like softly textured textiles, thickly padded carpets, windows with lovely treatments, and lots of pillows and throws. Not only are they cozy and comfortable, they also help create a hushed atmosphere. Peace and quiet are often all we want from the place we call home.

To ensure that unwanted noises are lessened and that pleasing ones are heightened, we must think about sound at the start of the design process. A house's configuration—the decisions about which rooms go where, and what they'll be adjacent to—determines the aural landscape. Putting closets between bedrooms is a good idea, for example, because it creates a sound buffer, while placing a fitness room or children's playroom above a master suite or home office is best avoided.

Even after a house is framed, you can control noise by using a variety of different soundproofing materials in walls and between floors. Fabrics, carpets, and special QuietRock all absorb sound, too, while double-paned windows and doors with glass that's a quarter- rather than an eighth-inch thick will do wonders for blocking unwanted noises from outside. You can go even further, and in ways that have distinctive aesthetic advantages. Upholstered walls provide some of the best sound-deadening available, and they add a pleasingly warm and tactile surface to a room, one that can be further embellished with such details as nail heads, tapes, and other trimmings. Wood can also absorb sound, and I've frequently used it on ceilings in a way that helps minimize noise in a room while simultaneously adding texture and detail.

Some rooms require more noise control than others. A quiet master bedroom ensures a good night's sleep, but the hushed environment created by soundproofing also leads to an atmosphere of safety and intimacy. That's a feeling you want not just in a master suite but in any bedroom, as well as dining rooms, bathrooms, studies, and media rooms. Other spaces may call for a more raucous atmosphere. Clanging pots, pans, and hands on marble or granite in a kitchen and family room feel festive and exciting, as does the vibrant sound of kids talking and singing in their bedroom or playroom.

When thinking about sound as one of the seven elements that give a place atmosphere, it's not just about keeping things quiet and deadening noise. We also want to amplify as much as possible all those laughs and giggles, hoots and hollers that give a home life and joy.

Each type of space plays a different role in our homes. This family room was meant to be an insulated lair in which to escape the world while enjoying a romantic movie or cheering a favorite sports team. Wood paneling, soft upholstery, and wool Roman shades ensure that no sound from the outside world gets into this space, and that none created inside it gets out.

You can tell right away when you've walked into a room with great acoustics: It has a different tenor, a different sense of echo and reverberation. It feels private, safe, and intimate, freeing you to be yourself.

This bedroom draws its sense of calm solace not only from its pale, low-contrast color palette, but also from the noise-dampening materials that cocoon it: the sound-baffling beams on the ceiling, the thick textiles used for upholstery and curtains, and the QuietRock on the walls.

A big, solid upholstered bed—especially one with a wingback headboard—provides an important assist when it comes to controlling noise, as do down duvets and mattress pads, layers of full curtains, and ceilings filled with sound-insulating material.

PART II

ATMOSPHERE *at Home*

The theory behind the seven elements of great design is one thing, but its realization is quite another. The following chapters look at how I have used these elements to create atmosphere in five different residences. In each, the seven elements simplified the design process even as they enlivened and emboldened the results, making these houses more extraordinary.

When working on these five homes, and the rooms within them, I considered every element singularly but also together. Doing so allows the elements to work in concert, and it allows the dwelling to have a better, more unified outcome, its various spaces flowing seamlessly from one to the next.

These residences demonstrate not only how the seven elements work together to create atmosphere, but also how atmosphere will make a house feel like home—a lovely and functional environment, made up of multiple and different rooms that comprise a cohesive whole.

MODERN CLASSIC

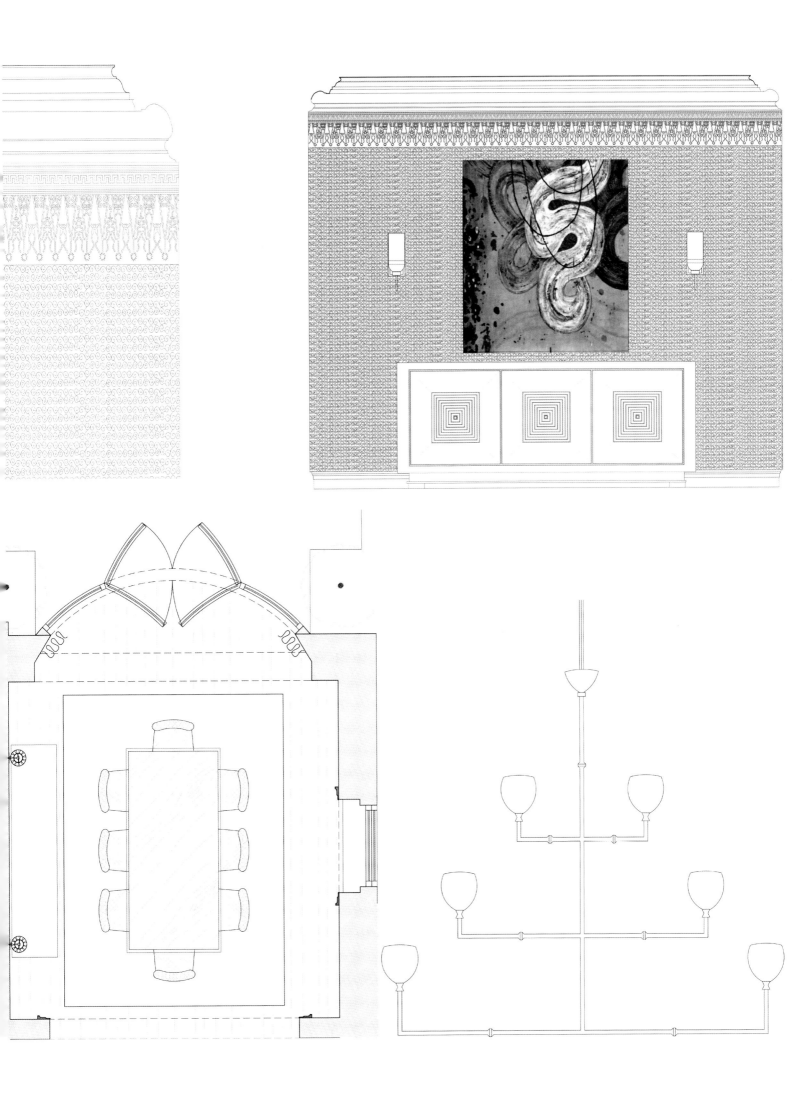

The owners of this remarkable property reached out to me for help reimagining their 1920s Colonial revival in upstate New York's Westchester County. They'd raised a family of four children within its grandly scaled, beautifully detailed spaces, and they felt ready to redecorate for the first time in decades.

The original design—with rooms of damask, arrangements of gilt furniture, and various Aubusson and Savonnerie carpets—took inspiration from eighteenth-century Europe. The aesthetic was opulent, to be sure, but it was a bit outdated. The homeowners wanted a change; they just weren't sure how to achieve it.

They knew they'd like something fresh, with a more modern sensibility, yet they also wanted to remain true to the building's roots as an important, classic American country house. Rather than sticking to a strictly Colonial idiom, however, they thought the home could instead surprise and delight with broader global inspiration, handcrafted details, and unique juxtapositions of traditional and contemporary furniture and art.

My earliest experience of the house occurred soon after the couple hired me. I came up to Westchester in the dead of winter one morning in February, when the daylight hours still felt far too short and the temperatures outside far too frigid—especially for a guy from Florida. The owners and I sat together by a roaring fire in the library, and they asked me what I'd do to achieve their lofty goals for the home.

Maybe it was the snow and ice I saw through the windows, but I immediately began thinking of Scandinavia. I realized that a lovely sense of Northern European light and a Swedish color palette in pale colors and other neutral hues would provide just the surprising but sophisticated atmosphere they craved. It would be cozy and familiar while also offering a certain formality, and it would remain in keeping with the building's classical bones, its robust scale and proportion, and its rich original details.

The house had large windows and got a fair bit of light, but it was still dark. We needed to lighten up the place, both literally, by letting in more sun and air, and figuratively, by relieving it from some of the weight it carried as a result of its heavy curtains, carpets, and color choices, as well as its monumental architecture. Against a refreshed, enlivened backdrop, the contemporary art and furnishings we would introduce could truly sing.

I began describing this vision by bringing the couple out of the library and into the adjacent foyer. "I think this could be like Sweden," I told them. "When you visit houses there, you notice that, whether they have lots of natural light or not, they manage to create as much bright, happy space as possible." The homeowners were intrigued. How would I do this, they wanted to know.

The hall's George II–style mirror, repainted a dark silvery gray, strikes a subtle note, almost becoming one with the surface of the deeply hued, hand-painted mural. Light on its feet, the diminutive console table doesn't distract from the surroundings.

In the foyer, profound classical architecture proves beautifully at peace with the more modern and delicately scaled black commode and painting by Ellsworth Kelly. The Gustavian blue wall color, combined with the glowing light and intricate moldings, creates a warm Swedish atmosphere.

THIS PAGE AND FOLLOWING PAGES:
Throughout the house, rich architectural details like pilasters and cornices are newly joined by clean-lined furnishings that have a classical sensibility despite a predominantly modern provenance. In the living room, a French corner sofa grounds shelves filled with Danish bisque vessels, while the walls are covered with a custom textured paper embossed with drawings by Mariano Fortuny and then glazed with translucent washes.

97

Rhythm calms
the mood and
pleases the eye,
but a feeling of
asymmetry keeps
things interesting
in a room.

The Cindy Sherman photograph over the
black bolection mantelpiece centers the
living room. The complex mix of furniture and
objects is unified by the repeated use of
gilt and bronze accents and the quiet, neutral
palette, which allows the grandeur of the
architecture to remain prominent.

I started simply. I walked to the doors at either end of the foyer and opened them to the outside, letting daylight pour in. And then I walked into the adjacent dining room and pulled open the heavy curtains there. "Let's lighten these window treatments," I said, "and switch out those solid wood doors for ones made largely of glass." Immediately, the foyer will feel immensely brighter—and, as a result, completely different.

"Then," I continued, "we'll lacquer the ceiling in pale ice blue to complement the polished dark green and white marble floor. Those shiny surfaces will reflect and bounce the light everywhere." The intricately carved, classical cornice moldings, architraves, and paneled wainscoting can be flat and chalk painted, with a stippled dado and base done as faux marbre. In contrast to these smooth, reflective surfaces, linen will cover the walls above the wainscoting, creating a modern, matte texture, and we'll paint the linen the perfect shade of Gustavian blue to achieve that Swedish feeling. It's an ideal backdrop for twentieth- and twenty-first-century art.

For the long, windowless hallway leading from the entryway to the light-filled living room, I suggested turning the lack of sun into a virtue, embracing the darkness between the two brighter spaces. We'd commission a hand-painted mural in moody, mysterious hues of loden green, silvery gray, and spruce, with lush flowers and birds depicted in a watery, jungle-like landscape. It would look like it was centuries old even though it was brand new.

In the pilastered living room at the far end of this corridor, the sense of scale and light would expand once more, thanks to high ceilings, four sets of French doors with transoms, and two additional windows flanking the fireplace. Here, an ivory palette now pervades, serving as a neutral canvas for bold contemporary art—including a Cindy Sherman self-portrait over the mantel—and seductively curvaceous seating upholstered in silk velvet. In keeping with the light, the space feels airy, lean, and spare. The room's richness comes from its mix of plush materials and textiles: soft velvets and woven fabrics, a bespoke wall covering whose pale pattern is printed on handmade paper, and a custom hand-woven silk-and-wool carpet in a subtle, low-contrast Moroccan pattern. Around the room, lustrous accents—a brass console with mid-century lines, a contemporary coffee table, a mirror in French Rococo style—add a lovely rhythm to a symmetrically balanced space.

The master suite is a world apart, in its own private wing. It is also something of a stylistic departure: a showplace for the couple's extraordinary collection of Art Deco furniture by Émile-

OPPOSITE: In the dining room, walls upholstered in velvet dampen sound, cultivating a hushed, private atmosphere and providing texture. The tea-paper ceiling reflects light from the mid-century Italian chandelier, bringing a celebratory sparkle to evening dinner parties. A classical sensibility defines the furnishings, as well as new millwork that reflects the original moldings elsewhere in the house. FOLLOWING PAGES: Colorful accents enliven the otherwise calm and demure dining room with a dose of the unexpected. A shell-topped niche displays a curated collection of Danish glass from the 1950s through the 1970s, and a work by Marc Chagall hangs over a Diego Giacometti–style console table.

This area previously comprised three small rooms. Now, the space holds a single large family-friendly chef's kitchen that nods to the home's 1920s Colonial revival origins. Simple, white-slab doors have a modern edge detail, and polished-nickel pulls were installed horizontally for a sculptural twist. The stainless steel appliance cabinets resemble massive armoires, while the milk glass in the upper cabinetry feels unexpected yet classic.

Jacques Ruhlmann and other makers of the period. The bedroom's and sitting room's new cabinetry and paneling are lacquered Macassar ebony, replicating the ebonized and polished surfaces of the exquisite Art Deco furniture in the suite and elsewhere in the house. The texture of the wall treatments offers contrast: In the bedroom, I created a grid of overlapping waxed-vellum sheets; in the sitting room, I commissioned a mural inspired by the work of French modernist artist Fernand Léger and the architect Le Corbusier, both contemporaries of Ruhlmann's.

Though the master suite sits separately, it still manages to flow from the rest of the house. I achieved this by maintaining the same sense of scale, proportion, and light found elsewhere. It also helps that additional Art Deco and mid-century items dot the house, such as the 1920s French rosewood-and-satinwood sideboard in the silver-leaf-ceilinged formal dining room.

Texture, too, serves as a through line. In the casual dining room just off the kitchen, I upholstered the walls in a sound-dampening ivory-and-sepia linen fabric whose pattern resembles an African mud cloth or an Indian block print. I used the same textile for the curtains along the room's curving wall of windows and French doors, effectively wrapping the entire space in it. These textured surfaces play against the smooth polish of the oak dining table by Wendell Castle and the French mid-century sideboard, which have a similar simplicity of line, despite being constructed thirty-five years apart.

Back in the library where the idea of Sweden first struck me, I reorganized the built-in shelving and cabinetry, then finished the paneling and millwork with a mottled, layered finish of another cool, soothing robin's egg Gustavian blue hue.

As I worked on these interiors, I carefully considered the character of the existing residence, trying to channel what the architect was thinking when he first designed it, and then combining that with the homeowners' desire for something fresh and new. Today, even though every space has been completely redecorated, the classical, Colonial revival aesthetic remains. The idea was to stay true to the original spirit of the house, but to craft new aspects that look and feel interesting and exciting. Working in parallel or related styles, albeit more modern ones, and picking pieces that seemed to speak the same language—that had the same sense of scale and proportion to each other—allowed me to marry these various aspects together.

This house has an unspoiled beauty as part of its existing exterior and interior architecture, and that endures as an important part of the remastered design and decor. That beauty just had to be newly appreciated and then imaginatively elevated.

The atmosphere of the casual dining room, next to the kitchen, comes from its many rich textures: the ribbed chenille upholstery of the chairs; the jute and wool of the micro-chevron carpet; the chipped white-plaster of the Diego Giacometti–style light fixture; and the wonderfully knobby, hand-blocked linen fabric on the walls, which is complemented by a primitive border sewn under the cornice.

Nothing contributes to a space's sense of calm quite like fabric-upholstered walls. They make a room feel like a sanctuary. Their power to insulate and absorb sound is so profound, you notice the hushed sense of quiet right away.

The lovely and diverse textures of the casual dining room are even more beautiful when sun from the bow-front French doors and sidelights dances across the woven fabrics on the walls, chairs, and floor and reflects off the French cabinet from the 1940s and the polished wood dining table designed by Wendell Castle in the 1980s.

The idea of introducing a Swedish
sensibility to this house originally
came from spending time in its
library in the middle of winter.
The owners asked how they might
make the space brighter and
happier, which led to the proposal
of using pale glazed and over-
painted Gustavian colors and
washes to embrace the Northern
European–like light.

112

THIS PAGE: If you look closely at very old finishes in great houses or on furniture, you'll notice they have something in common: layers and layers of washes of transparent pigment. This patina was mimicked in the previously darkly stained library. A newly added chandelier, bookcase lighting, and sconces at the mantel further brighten the room, resulting in an evenly and atmospherically lit space that can be used equally well during the day or at night. FOLLOWING PAGES: The master suite was conceived to highlight the owners' impressive collection of Art Deco furniture by Frenchman Émile-Jacques Ruhlmann. His drawing room at 1925's Paris Exposition featured a powerful and dramatic mural that served as a magnificent backdrop for his avant-garde designs. This sitting room took that as inspiration, but in a quieter, more subtle way, because of its natural light and intimate scale. It immediately envelops you in an atmosphere of calm and beauty.

PREVIOUS PAGES: The homeowners' Art Deco furniture was the impetus for the scheme of this serene and subdued room, where a recessed niche sheathed in Macassar ebony matches the bed's frame. The true focal point, however, is the painting by Jean Dunand over the chaise. The subtle bouclé carpet, supple wool curtains, and waxed-paper wall covering keep all eyes on the artwork. ABOVE: With its exquisitely outfitted cabinets and paneling, the master suite's closet channels the look of the iconic Deco-era ship the *Normandie*. In homage to that cruiser—and in keeping with the Ruhlmann-adorned bedroom and sitting room nearby—the steamer trunk–inspired setting uses Macassar ebony, mirrored stainless steel, and leather. OPPOSITE: The modern scheme of the reimagined master bath features a marble mosaic floor pattern in an Art Deco design. Because of the limited natural light, everything remains pale in color and polished, the better to extract as much luster and reflection as possible.

ALONG THE WATERFRONT

When homeowners trust their designer enough to give him a good bit of freedom to run with his ideas—to decorate their house in the manner he thinks will suit it and them best—the result can be a dream. But such liberty can also be a curse: With it comes the understanding that the project will be wildly ambitious, and entirely successful, because to whom much is given, much is expected. This newly built estate on a former farm in Water Mill, in New York's Hamptons, thankfully managed to surpass expectations.

The place was to be a modern-day getaway for an urban couple who would use it to host children and grandchildren and entertain friends in groups big and small. To design it, I worked with Atlanta-based architect Peter Block, someone I've enjoyed collaborating with many times before. We share a strong appreciation for classical architecture, a love and understanding of its potential for beauty, and a belief that even the grandest of homes should feel human scaled. We also both love bold, dramatic gestures—something this house has in spades.

Because of its quiet, peaceful position—far away from any roads, on three rolling acres overlooking Mecox Bay and the Atlantic Ocean, with five more acres of open land on either side—we conceived the property as an English country house with magnificent public rooms and big open porches. We wanted it to make a statement, so we designed it with inspiration from late-nineteenth- and early-twentieth-century British neoclassical architect Edwin Lutyens, who designed heroic houses that were big but didn't feel sprawling.

Since this home is in the Hamptons, not the Cotswolds, we wanted it to be sympathetic to the vernacular architecture of Long Island's East End. We departed from the British idiom here and there—notably on the exterior, which we clad in cedar shakes rather than English stone—adding elements of the area's traditional shingle style. Inside, we created a classical, largely symmetrical plan, its voluminous rooms opening off wide hallways on both the ground floor and upper level. Many spaces directly connect from one to the next through broad openings aligned on a single axis, allowing enfilade views through the length of the house.

The scale throughout is statement-making: Ceilings rise a minimum of twelve feet; hallways extend to a width of ten feet; and windows, which face largely south in the lively public quarters and north in the quieter bedrooms, stand ten feet tall. All told, between its

Seen as a way simply to get from here to there, hallways are often devoid of interesting features, if not downright dull. But the grandeur of the proportions of the corridors in this home—which takes its cues from the great country houses of England—matches those of its antecedents: Each hallway is nearly ten feet wide, with tall ceilings and massive, thickened arches that nearly touch the cornice. Large-scale pendant lights complement these proportions, as does the bold wall mural.

seven en-suite bedrooms and various living and entertaining rooms, the home offers 12,000 square feet of living area. But its atmosphere feels profoundly warm and intimate. The house never overwhelms its inhabitants with its magnitude.

This generously sized residence feels friendly and welcoming, even downright cozy, because the interior design and decor remain as robust as the scale and proportion of the rooms and the building itself. To ensure that no space would seem cool or austere, dramatic decorative elements and striking architectural details abound. In this home—unlike a smaller, timid one— the moldings had to be far more three-dimensionally shaped, the colors had to be more intense, the patterns more graphic, and the finishes and textiles more distinctive. As simple and clean-lined as they are, the furniture needed to be bold, too, with tall canopy beds, long sofas, and ample armchairs. Even the doorknobs here are big.

Nothing, however, is ever out of scale or out of proportion. Instead, the many decorative elements are each properly sized in relation to the architecture, and that's why it all works together so very well.

Consider the commodious living room. Its heavily beamed ceiling soars to twenty-three feet, creating a truly capacious volume. But you don't feel as if you're getting lost in the space, because the ivory-painted wood paneling that wraps the room ends right at the height where the second story begins, just above the doors. This breaks down the elevation of the room, making it feel human-scaled. Running the paneling all the way to the ceiling would have emphasized its verticality, and the spirit would have been entirely different. Instead, above the paneled walls, paints and glazes in various muted shades of sky blue, taupe, and sepia create a dynamic, layered finish atop sand-textured plaster. Those walls are meant to look as if they had been chipping and flaking paint for three hundred years.

The bravado continues into the furnishings. The pattern of the custom rug is based on the shapes in Henri Matisse's cutouts, which were scanned and then fashioned into a large-scale design whose low-contrast grays and beiges mitigate its boldness. On top were placed such substantial pieces as a seven-by-three-foot live-edge fruitwood coffee table and immense shelter-style sofa. Above it all hangs a light sculpture by David Weeks that calls to mind the mobiles of Alexander Calder.

PREVIOUS PAGES: Welcoming guests with a light and lively atmosphere, the foyer features curving sky-blue lacquered walls and a boldly patterned polished marble floor designed to reflect the glow of sunlight from the front door, sidelights, and bay window above. OPPOSITE: Two-story spaces can easily overwhelm, but this living room appears lower than it actually is, thanks to the large wooden panels that stop at the floor height of the second story. Enhancing the human scale, the furniture is soft and comfortable, set in cozy arrangements that entice you to come in and sit. While the custom-designed handmade carpet is based on Henri Matisse's cutouts and the chandelier nods to Alexander Calder's mobiles, there's relatively little art on the walls; the textural finishes are so profound, little more was needed.

In his book *On Decorating*, Mark Hampton discusses what he calls the "look through": what you see when you gaze from one room to the next. Adjacent rooms need to unfold in an intentional way, with each offering something new. Here the massive features and coarse textures of the living room are slightly contrasting the smaller scaled and more edited kitchen surfaces.

The bedrooms are equally grand and roomy but also private and secluded. When guests stay, they should all feel as if they've gotten upgrades to the best room in the house. The atmosphere is kept cozy in these spaces in several different ways. Each chamber has its own vestibule, which provides a layer of privacy and a sense of anticipation before you enter the primary space. In some quarters, canopy beds anchor the room; in others, conversation-conducive sitting areas nestle within the larger space. In all cases, the walls and ceiling are embellished with surprising finishes and details to add intriguing textural moments.

Because of the house's views across the lawn, gardens, and bay to the ocean, the palette that arose was based largely on greens and blues. Some of the colors are quite saturated; others less so. Hues of ivory and sage, as well as intense blue and violet, fill the house with warmth, complementing the other elements of the design. Their particular values, shades, and tones provide a beauty and loveliness that is more a murmur than a shout. The rich green-patterned fabric used on the walls and for the curtains in the dining room, for example, reflects what you see from the windows in that space, while the dark blue of the sound-dampening fabric on the walls and the Roman shades in the media room recalls the Hamptons' midnight skies, suggesting romantic evenings. The earthy, chestnut-colored lacquered walls of the master suite's sitting room are capped by a massive modillion block cornice lacquered a shade darker. The low contrast is both quiet and interesting—just the feeling you want in a space conceived as a sanctuary for its owners.

Every room of this house tells a different, but equally compelling, story. To make this possible, a particular feature of the design advances in one space, and then another aspect becomes primary in the next. Take the living room: there, the rich texture of the multicolored scratch-coat plaster on the upper walls especially catches the eye, while in the adjacent foyer, it's the ceiling, with its lustrous lacquer, that becomes the focus. This variation allows for new experiences as you move through the house, all of which is tied together with certain commonalities of design: bold and unique

THIS PAGE AND PREVIOUS PAGES: The library was meant to have a particularly private, masculine atmosphere, its walls sheathed in warm, textured vellum, the millwork faux-grained to resemble walnut, and the Jean-Michel Frank–style sofa upholstered in soft velvet. These rich materials and surfaces harmonize with the intricate Richard Giglio painting hung over the sofa, which came from the owner's collection. The bronze side tables are by Jacques Garcia, while the chairs are custom.

134

yet familiar materials and features, as well as lots of pattern, predominantly in low-contrast or otherwise subtle colorways. The scale is huge, but also decidedly human, and the style of the furnishings mixes some wonderful nineteenth-century Continental antiques with more modern and mid-century pieces.

There's a lot going on here, but it's never too much, because each room is a different interpretation of these qualities and the atmosphere they create. My reverence for the great houses I have so frequently visited in the countryside of England helped me stay on course. The best of those British residences, no matter how large and how full of precious possessions, manage to feel like embodiments of an individual's desire to live life in comfort and style. Their owners were educated and wise custodians who filled their walls with extraordinary artwork, their rooms with beautiful furniture gathered on travels around the world, and their shelves with interesting books acquired over the course of generations. Their spaces, like those of this house, feel privileged and luxurious, cultivated and curated, but at the same time comfortable, often even informal, and enriched with the right details for the right reasons.

THIS PAGE AND PREVIOUS PAGES: The luxurious feeling of the media room springs largely from the rich, unique midnight blue color of the upholstered wall, whose mix of matte and lustrous yarns is woven in a small geometric pattern. The intense shade of the wall fabric and the padding behind it create the ideal environment for watching movies in the dark and in silence. The various super-soft textures of the upholstery textiles beg you to get cozy in the sofas and armchairs; their pale color pops against the saturated backdrop.

THIS PAGE AND PREVIOUS PAGES: The dining room takes its stylistic direction from the great late-nineteenth-century houses designed on Long Island by the firm of McKim, Mead & White. The views of the sunny landscaped grounds, the bay, and the ocean from the nearly floor-to-ceiling windows, meanwhile, led the design not only to its green-and-blue color palette but also to its garden trellis–like quatrefoil tracery ceiling moldings.

PREVIOUS PAGES: Maintaining a consistently clean and spare sensibility, the kitchen shows off the beauty of sleek and smooth materials and finishes—stainless steel, white lacquer, polished nickel, and ribbed glass. The lacquered ceiling reflects the light from the south-facing windows, giving the space an extra sense of liveliness. THIS PAGE: A limited color palette and contrasting textures prove a winning combination in the master suite's sitting room. Mocha lacquered walls and dark cinnamon lacquered moldings set off the textured, relatively pale upholstery fabrics as well as the carpet, whose raised fretwork pattern becomes more apparent as light from a nearby window plays over it.

The atmosphere of the master bedroom is one of indulgence, hushed calm, and absolute privacy. Wood-paneled walls painted a soft ivory wrap the space in a warm texture and provide a sense of order to what might otherwise have felt like just another big room. The fabrics used have a soft, sumptuous hand, while the custom faux-bois carpet serves to ground the entire space with lovely dark color and bold pattern.

ABOVE: The overdoor transoms of eighteenth-century England inspired the design of the foyer's spiderweb oculus, which allows the sun to filter down into the space. **OPPOSITE:** Subtle contrasts of tone are key to the quiet, serene sensibility of this guest bedroom retreat, where combed walls in multiple shades of green, blue, gray, and ivory easily blend with the custom floral rug. A monochrome paint treatment softens the bold geometry of the patterned wood ceiling.

ABOVE: Successfully using texture in a room means mixing materials. When there is contrast, each surface is better appreciated. In this dressing room, the block pattern of the wooden walls has a more profound effect because of the smoothness of the pale-blue ceiling. **OPPOSITE:** In the billiard room, a formal, classical cornice, whose rondels whimsically mimic pool balls, plays off the relatively humble material on the walls: plywood squares arranged in a grid and washed with several coats of paint.

A HAMPTONS HOME

My wife, Phoebe, and I first came to the Hamptons over a July Fourth weekend. We flew up from Florida to stay with old friends in a nineteenth-century clapboard house in the village of East Hampton, within biking distance of Main Beach and the Atlantic Ocean and many restaurants and boutiques. Simply put, we loved every aspect of the area: The air was clear and clean and cool, especially when compared with Jacksonville in mid-summer; the carefully landscaped gardens were perfect; and the classical architecture of the homes struck a chord with our Southern sensibilities. It felt like the Hamptons had all the romantic old-fashioned charms of centuries-old villages in the Northeast while offering the best of nearly everything, from gourmet cuisine and farm-to-table produce to interesting shops and antiques galleries. We returned to visit our friends several times that summer, and the following season, we came up to see them even more. We were hooked.

Years later, we finally bought a house of our own, not far from that first one we'd stayed in, and we gradually started to become locals. When we sold that one, it was only a matter of time before we started thinking about how to get ourselves back. We did so with this home.

I found the perfect lot, in an area I call "the center of the universe" because it seems like the very middle of Long Island's South Fork, with easy access to all points north, south, east, and west. The particular plot of land sits back from the road, at the end of a long drive and overlooking a largely open twenty-five-acre parcel of land. With all this air around it, the site feels quiet, protected, and very private. And I wanted the home—which I conceived as our dream house—to have a similar atmosphere.

To make the dream a reality, I turned to Atlanta-based architect Bobby McAlpine, who has been celebrated for years for his Mannerist-style exteriors. I asked Bobby for a seven-bedroom home that would have lots of space to gather with our family and friends: a large, central, multifunctional living area for hosting groups; a chef's kitchen whose table could easily seat twelve people; a TV room with a fireplace; and ample area downstairs for playing games and hanging out. Each bedroom would have its own bathroom, and the master suite would include its own seating area as well as another fireplace.

I didn't want it to feel like a big house, however. Instead, it was meant to have a sense of intimacy: rooms that were human-scaled, most ceilings no more than ten feet in height, and lots

A successfully designed entry sequence will intrigue you and make you want to explore the rest of a house. This one is full of unexpected colors, patterns, and textures, including that of a contemporary bronze torso by Isabelle Melchior. The flag artwork by Tom Dash in the hallway beyond is made of a repeated image of supermodel Kate Moss printed in red, white, and blue.

of natural light from big windows. As for the architectural aesthetic, I commissioned Bobby to create something in the shingle style, with a romantic feeling. I was looking to have old New England meet a Scottish farmhouse, with the texture and sense of whimsy of swooping rooflines, the interplay of cedar shakes set against stone, and large expanses of glass. We wanted roof symmetry as well, with a fireplace in each corner and one in the center, their chimneys poking through the roof.

What Bobby designed was a classic "four part," its double-height central living space surrounded by smaller rooms in the corners: the kitchen, family TV room, master suite, and study on the ground floor, plus four bedrooms above. This sort of symmetrical plan can sometimes feel formal, but we counteracted that by playing with tradition. We tucked the second-story rooms up into the roof rafters, creating large, airy, light-filled volumes, and we developed a sense of rhythm in each space, making sure that fireplaces were slightly off center and openings for doorways and windows were syncopated. There's order and balance to be sure, but no exact symmetry. These quirks and irregularities make the place feel less formal and more fun.

It takes a while after you move into a house for it to feel like your home, even for people like Phoebe and me, who both have a bit of a nomadic gene. You usually need some time to bond with a place, to get it to fit you like a comfortable pair of shoes or a favorite old chair. But we bonded with this one right away. This was thanks in large part to that mantra of "less formal, more fun," which guided the interior and helped define its atmosphere. The house is both warm and wow-inducing. It is private but at the same time welcoming, filled with joy, happiness, and, increasingly, some of our fondest memories.

The house's sense of atmosphere begins from the moment you enter it. Although petite and somewhat dark, the foyer is full of texture, sound, and, as a result, vibrant life. Sandy marmorino plaster on the walls sits against lacquered carved moldings and polished marble floors inlaid with a graphic geometric pattern. The art—a thickly painted oil-on-canvas and a rough-hewn bronze torso—continues the tactile story. These hard surfaces let the sounds of joyful greetings penetrate deep into the house, the laughs and shouts of friends echoing front to back, up and down.

PREVIOUS PAGES: In the home's grandly scaled living room, a fittingly enormous painting by Caio Fonseca captures the eye. Sun from the north- and south-facing clerestory and the walls of windows below fills the double-height space with an almost celestial glow, while the soft handmade lamb's wool carpet is a treat for bare feet.
OPPOSITE: Arrangements of paintings, sculptures, and furnishings with interesting silhouettes and textures lend a sense of rhythm to this gallery alcove on the north side of the living room. A Gilbert Poillerat–style steel library table sits in front of a low Brutalist buffet, adjacent to a nineteenth-century Danish cabinet.

ABOVE: In the living room, the Tudor-style Portland stone mantel adds another monumental element to the high-ceilinged space. The smooth but hard materials—bronze, stone, and iron—against a wall covering of handmade paper work wonderfully together. OPPOSITE: The contemporary painting is alive with so much pattern and color, it feels electrified. The warm neutrals of the surrounding decor prove the perfect backdrop for the artwork's robust design and cool tones.

I like to think of a house as unfolding in front of you, with the experience of each space different than the one before. In the case of this home, from the foyer, you can already see the light and liveliness of the double-height main space, and that draws you in, through an entrance hall, to the heart of the home. This central room—which impresses with its clerestory, faux-grained wood columns, oak trusses, massive Portland stone fireplace, and tiered iron Diego Giacometti–style chandeliers—sets the stage, and in many ways, the design scheme, for the rest of the house. Both here and throughout, I used the highest quality, honest natural materials and furnishings: things that are beautiful and refined, rich and lovely to see and touch, but not elegant or dear. They don't say, "I'm expensive," or "Look at me." Instead, they feel relaxed, and they're made to be used. You want to sit in every chair or sofa, and the practically minded, hard-working (and hard-to-destroy) leathers and wools, linens, and woods can all be cleaned easily. The floors have wire-brushed limed and antiqued finishes that only minimally show dirt and scratches. The idea is one of comfort and warmth.

This extends to the palette of golden beiges, ecrus, sages, taupes, and ciel and cornflower blues. They're all different experiences of the idea of neutral, with bolder color coming from robust artworks, like the Jim Dine in the study, the Keith Haring in the kitchen, and the Caio Fonseca over the mantel in the central space.

Beyond that main room, in the corners of the house, the scale and proportion contract back down to something more intimate. The study's limed-oak paneled walls, hand-woven nubby rug, and chenille-like textiles, for example, embrace everyone who enters. Upstairs, I added drama to the cozy corner guest bedrooms by finishing the peaked ceiling of each with a different shingle-style–inspired beamed treatment. These rooms' relatively small size, as well as their rich and soft textures and the fact that the proportion of every decorative element is in keeping with its overall scale, ensures that these spaces seem like hushed sanctuaries, especially when juxtaposed with the sense of expansion and exuberance of the home's central block.

Phoebe and I have found that our guests have come to feel about this house the same way we felt about the Hamptons after our initial visit all those years ago: After being here once, you want to come back to stay again and again.

The intricate texture of the Diego Giacometti–inspired cast-bronze étagères dances with movement, shadows, and highlights. Its hammered appearance offers a counterpoint to the handmade Danish pottery displayed on the glass shelves, highlighting the smooth, curving forms of the glazed ceramics.

ABOVE: A Japanese jar sits atop a porphyry pedestal in the corner of the dining room, providing balance—without perfect symmetry—to the painting hung on the other side of the doorway.
OPPOSITE: The strong, clean lines and dark color of the dye-stained oak dining table anchor the otherwise airy volume of this barrel-vaulted, pale-hued, sunlit space.

166

This salon treats the eye to an assortment of objects whose shimmering surfaces play against adjacent materials that are more matte. Not only do the round blue mirror, platinum-leaf cocktail table, and various polished-stone pieces catch the direct sun that pours in from the enormous window, they also reflect the light that bounces off the gold tea-paper ceiling.

168

ABOVE: A simple nineteenth-century Italian octagonal mirror and modern, polished-nickel sconces let the rosso levanto marble sink base hold pride of place in the powder room. With its lovely luster and intense veining, the vanity is opulent but not aggressive. OPPOSITE: A double-height window throws the soft spiral of the winding staircase into silhouette as it ascends to the second floor—it may feel a bit theatrical, but then drama is often what atmosphere is all about.

PREVIOUS PAGES: Very few materials bring warmth to a space like wood paneling, especially when it features a molded architrave, base, and cornices. The wool shades, linen sofa, and leather cocktail ottoman offer a soft, welcoming embrace to anyone who enters the sitting room. ABOVE: On the mantel, seemingly disparate objects—a contemporary vase, a more traditional glazed-ceramic bird figurine, and a minimalist-modern monolithic porcelain prism—rest nicely together, thanks to their shared color palette and similar textures. OPPOSITE: A work on paper by Hans Hoffman hangs above a console that takes its cues from Diego Giacometti; the two creatives worked during the same period at the middle of the twentieth century, which helps this vignette cohere.

Once considered "back-of-house" or "below-stairs" spaces, kitchens are now the center of our everyday lives and of every special event we host, and they're designed accordingly. This one—with its scrim-glass-fronted cabinets, custom stainless-steel-and-brass oven hood, marble counters, and sculptural light fixture—stands as profound proof that what used to be banal and utilitarian has evolved to become imaginative and sophisticated.

What's more romantic in a bedroom than a fireplace? It's especially easy to cozy up to when you use a gas flame that can be turned on at the touch of a button.

In the sitting area of the master bedroom, the cut-stone mantel sits amid soft, quiet neutral hues of ecru, stone, and sand. Painted wood paneling frames the fireplace and fills the space with warmth. Atop the mantel are five Coade stone jars, and hanging above is a custom Gerald Bland mirror whose rondels were formed from streetlight orbs.

The master bedroom serves as a fine example of how smartly mixing materials, and even furniture styles, can result in a successful scheme. Although diverse, all the fabrics used for the upholstery and bedding are made of fine natural fibers with a sensuous hand feel. As for the furnishings, a Black Forest armchair sits next to 1970s glass-and-Perspex bunching tables and adjacent to an Italian-style iron bed. The assorted provenances don't distract, however, because each piece is classically influenced and has similar proportions to the others.

PREVIOUS PAGES: The master bathroom is a study in the beauty of black, white, and gray marbles used together. Polished-mirror stainless steel trims the vanity's doors and drawers, while an inlay of white frosted glass highlights the mirror, echoing the sconces flanking it. The organic veining of the Carrara marble counters, wall cladding, and tub surround presents a striking juxtaposition to the rigid geometric pattern of the floor. THIS PAGE: Texture and rhythm take center stage in this guest room, where multiple patterns of ceiling beams combine with a linear wall covering whose pattern was flipped to create a checkerboard. Nail head details on the bed and armchair, a lattice-fronted French cabinet from the 1940s, and Mongolian lamb throw round out the tactile feeling.

PAGE 186: The irregular surface of a white plaster planter shows off the absolute smoothness of the amethyst glass and obelisk beside it. PAGE 187: No corner is left unadorned; here, a French mid-century miroir du soleil hangs above a semanier from the same period. THIS PAGE: Roof framing offers design opportunities. The trusses and beaming in the four soaring and spacious upstairs bedrooms of this house echo the timbered ceiling treatment of the living room. The millwork in each is different, but the repeated variations on a theme establish a consistency that helps create atmosphere.

Guest bedrooms should be some of the best spaces in a house. You want the friends and family who stay with you to leave thoroughly satisfied, well rested, and having been only too happy to make your home their own—even if only for a few days.

Romance is important in a bedroom, but so too are more practical considerations. Here, a high-backed headboard makes sitting up to read, watch TV, or work more comfortable, while the ample nightstand provides storage space, and the adjustable lamp gives focused task light. The mildly textured walls were painted with a lime-based green-tinged paint, then topped with a smoothing coat of wax.

ABOVE: Varying the art over the matched pair of mirrors and placing a single accent pillow on one side of the settee is all it takes to syncopate the rhythm of this otherwise perfectly symmetrical sitting area. The thick upholstery fabrics and deep carpet, and even the books on the shelves, absorb sound, making this a serene place to read. **OPPOSITE:** Barely-there hints of soft blue and light lavender in the fabrics lead to a feeling of subtle elegance in this blue-gray-walled guest room, where the scale of the upholstered partial canopy bed matches the dramatic weight of the ceiling beams.

THIS PAGE AND FOLLOWING PAGES: This groin-vaulted hallway on the lower level was designed to recall subterranean spaces in important European houses more than the typical American basement. The bold and sturdy furnishings, art, and objects—including a Gothic monastery table, an oversize bronze urn, a bas relief by Bunny Williams, a stone Italianate table, and plaster ceiling pendants—remind you that you are in a sort of fortress-like space with thick foundation walls and massive arches.

Bold proportions, heavenly light, and a playful take on tradition define this modern-day summer house in New York's Hamptons. Like many who come to this part of the world and ultimately build their dream houses here, this home's owners—a creatively minded Manhattan couple— required a residence that embodied the unique combination of relaxation and refinement that has long made the Hamptons a sought-after destination. They wanted a house with an atmosphere as casual as it was sophisticated, as convivial as it was secluded. They initially thought they needed a quiet, intimate escape where they could host family and friends over occasional weekends in the summer season. But during the years since the home's completion, they've come to spend more and more time here, with larger groups of people, using the property year-round and on weekdays, too, so enamored are they of its inviting and sun-filled spaces.

Set in a beach retreat enclave, their seven-bedroom, eight-bathroom house perches on a pastoral one-plus-acre parcel adjacent to farmland, with tall, old-growth linden and London plane trees on is periphery. This flat, largely open landscape means the home is blessed with beautiful unobscured light. Sun absolutely pours in during the day from the south, and there's ample illumination from the north, too. The quality of the light here became one of the residence's most defining characteristics, and it significantly affected how the other elements of great design combined to create atmosphere in the interiors.

Though it offers its occupants and their guests some 10,500 square feet of living space, the home wears its size lightly, dividing its area over three levels and veiling its volume in the area's vernacular shingle style of architecture. A certain asymmetry defines these often-sprawling, cedar-shake-covered houses, whose rooflines undulate with gables, dormers, and eyebrow windows, and whose porches and verandas can appear in delightfully surprising locations. Frequently rambling and rarely symmetrical, these buildings revel in the beauty of quirkiness, the fun of the informal and the rustic.

Much about the home's decoration proceeded from this shingle-style exterior, as I worked this iconic American idiom into the interior architecture throughout. Well-proportioned detailing adorns and defines each room. Highly articulated moldings, beamed ceilings, pilastered doorways, and paneled walls honor the sense of craft, artistry, and ornament that are hallmarks of the look.

THIS PAGE AND PREVIOUS PAGE: The foyer establishes
this light-filled home's radiant atmosphere,
which is defined by an imaginative reinterpretation
of tradition. Its scale is grand but the rooms
remain disciplined. Here, a classic diamond motif
was used for the marble floor's simple, geometric
pattern, and the lightness of the floating stair—
with its undulating S curves capped by oak stair
nosings—is an engineering enigma.

In keeping with the undulating asymmetry that defines the shingle style, I designed a series of rooms whose rhythmic scale and proportion progress from the cozy and petite to the grandly expansive and then back again. The larger spaces generally have decor with greater proportions, while the smaller ones have less.

After approaching the house along a bluestone path, one finds oneself on a small covered porch, its dimensions narrow in both directions, and its ceiling relatively short because the shed portion of the roof is low here. This space offers no real view of the surrounding landscape, and it gives an overall feeling of compression, but in a pleasant, cozy way that also creates a sense of anticipation.

From here, this portal entry gives way, through the simple front door, to a much wider and deeper foyer. There, a suspended staircase, with a rounded cyma-shaped bracket on the underside of each step, rises into a double-height space, stretching the expansion upward. Gleaming, lustrous surfaces—not least the lacquered pale-blue ceilings and polished gray and white marble floors—further add to the sense of volume, lightness, and brightness.

The furniture's proportions relate to the size of the room, but the extent of their boldness defies expectations, offering a surprising spin on tradition. The graphic, inset-diamond pattern of the marble floor, for example, is quite classic, but it was rendered here in a very large scale so it would feel more contemporary. Complementing this is the diameter of the pool-cue-shaped balustrades support-ing the handrail; these are wider than tradition might have them, but they will stand up to the graphic floor.

The same is true of the monumental, slab-style consoles that flank the foyer's opening to the living room. They hold their own against the floor pattern and under the bold artwork that hangs above each of them. Placing a single work by Richard Giglio over one table and a grid of nine brightly colored images over the other augments the room's rhythm, balancing the off-center placement of the steps.

PREVIOUS PAGES AND OPPOSITE: The dramatic living room sits in the center of the house, as the home's lively heart. A slight taper in the beams of the twenty-eight-foot ceiling adds lightness and refinement, which prevents the space from feeling barn-like. Augmenting the room's sophistication are the Fortuny pillows, Art Deco cabinet, and a linen sofa and buttery leather chairs attributed to Jean-Michel Frank. The cantilevered ceiling fixture is by David Weeks.

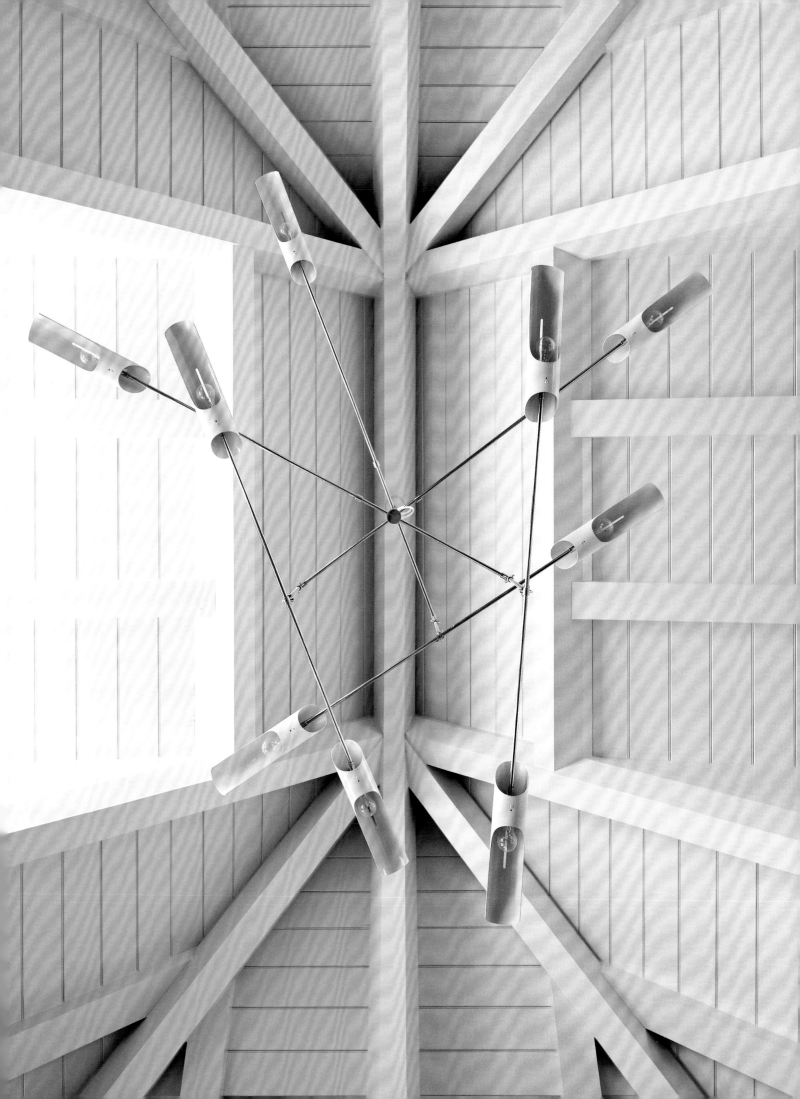

The rhythmic progression of scale and proportion from compression to expansion reaches its apex in the vast volume of the central living room, before shrinking again in the adjacent kitchen, dining room, and library, and then upstairs in the even more intimate bedrooms.

The grand living room, for its part, extends to a height of twenty-eight feet, culminating in a vaulted ceiling finished with planking and heavy beams that emphasize the soaring architecture of the space. Both the clerestory and eleven-foot-tall wall of windows and glass doors at the rear of the room ensure that this south-facing space is all about natural illumination.

The selection and placement of the furnishings keeps the focus on the element of light: The pieces are all relatively minimal and were arranged to enjoy the best possible sun from the windows, while floor lamps stand so that their shades sit between windows rather than in front of them.

The design of the living room celebrates the natural light that bathes the space. The seating sits within ample sun that pours in through three sets of glass doors surrounded by sidelights and transoms. Low-profile furniture lets light reach all across the room, without interruption.

Nothing creates shimmering effects and a glamorous atmosphere quite as well as a silver-leaf tea-paper ceiling—perfect for a festive and delicious meal.

The color palette works equally well with the property's impressive light. The suite of barely-there but very warm neutrals may at first appear almost monochromatic, but careful examination reveals a captivating variety within the beach-inspired pink-y tan, oatmeal, buff, and sand shades, as well as in the spruce greens, sages, celadons, and pale blues, all of which have slightly different intensities. This soothing scheme brings another dose of contemporary style to the home's classical elements.

A careful layering and juxtaposition of textures, meanwhile, produces a lovely envelope that heightens the atmosphere and elevates the experience of being in the home. Smooth plaster walls contrast with thick frieze carpet in the living room, for example, and fluted and recessed boiserie plays off a grid of sound-dampening fabric panels in the silver-leaf–ceilinged dining room.

In a residence with relatively limited variations in hue, texture becomes a profound way to expand the palette. This works particularly

In the dining room, fluted pilasters enhance the height, drawing the eye up to the cornice. In the middle of the ceiling, a circular, silver-leafed recess complements the shape of the vintage chandelier. The padded linen panels on the walls help attenuate sound, allowing dinner guests to hear each other across the custom vellum-covered table.
FOLLOWING PAGES: A photographic collage provides a dose of color to the otherwise neutral palette, while a Napoleon III–style mirror hangs over a French Art Deco enfilade. The mid-century–inspired dining chairs used throughout improve diners' comfort and happiness.

well in a light-filled home like this, because the sun helps show off what can be subtle differences between surface treatments. A study in textures, the library makes this fact abundantly clear. Its array of soft, nubby, natural textiles; its warm, richly grained woods; and its ribbed, cross-vaulted ceiling—based on one originally designed by Sir John Soane—create a sense of splendor, especially when seen in the light of day. This is also true in the bedrooms. The home's guest quarters see layers of natural materials like embroidered cotton and linen, and the beamed vaulted ceiling of the master suite offers a bold hit of texture overhead. The changes in that ceiling's height, from six and a half feet at the edges of the sitting area, to twelve feet over the bed, have the added benefit of allowing the space to be both intimate and expansive.

In this light-filled, classically chic home, the visual and tactile information contained in the interiors tantalizes the senses, yet there's no sense of information overload. That's the magic of atmosphere: What really jumps out at you is nothing; what you are aware of is everything. The feeling of perfect equilibrium comes about not because of any one thing—an individual piece of furniture or even one of the seven elements of great design—but because of the harmony achieved by the overall composition and by the careful use of all seven elements.

PREVIOUS PAGES: Using different materials and finishes for various components of a kitchen's design can add richness. Here, nearly everything is polished—including the walnut end cabinets—something that serves to energize the space. The finish of the rift-sawn oak flooring, however, is matte and dry textured. This contrast makes every one of the components stand on its own, highlighting the beauty of each. OPPOSITE: A spacious banquette pairs well with a series of small tables that can be pushed together or pulled apart; this keeps the setting appropriate for groups both big and small.

The library's large size and nearly perfectly square shape made it an ideal place for a ribbed, groin-vaulted ceiling treatment based on one originally designed by Sir John Soane. Placed in each corner, the large, classically inspired bookshelves—made of quartered and rift-sawn oak with a dry wax finish—visually anchor the vault to the floor, which is covered with a custom rug. The abstract painting's rich colors influenced the palette for the rest of the space.

218

Scale and proportion proved key to providing atmosphere here. Lowering the ceiling height around the perimeter and using a single custom wool-and-silk carpet to unite the sleeping and sitting areas make a very large master bedroom feel cozy. The room's symmetry, monochrome palette, and soft textures result in a sense of calm.

PAGE 222: From the embroidered Indian cotton of the bed curtains and valance to the waxed faux-python wall covering, everything about this guest bedroom feels smooth to the touch, fostering a mood of ease and quietude. PAGE 223: A wall of antiqued mirrors gently bounces welcoming light from a window opposite back into this bathroom, throwing sun around the space without the glare an ordinary mirror might cause. THIS PAGE: In this guest bedroom, a symmetrical grid of wood slatting organizes the rhythm of the space, disguising the fact that the doors and windows don't have ideal placement. The bed is upholstered in horizontal stripes to echo this newly articulated geometry, and a placid purple palette of low-contrast raisin, plum, and eggplant hues unites it all.

Mirrors are a necessity in a bathroom—but they also are a light-reflecting design opportunity. Here, large ones flank a mirrored door, while those set into the window jamb help sun enter the space. The polished nickel of the vanity legs, sink fixtures, and sconces adds to the rhythm of reflective surfaces around the room.

THE MODERN FARMHOUSE

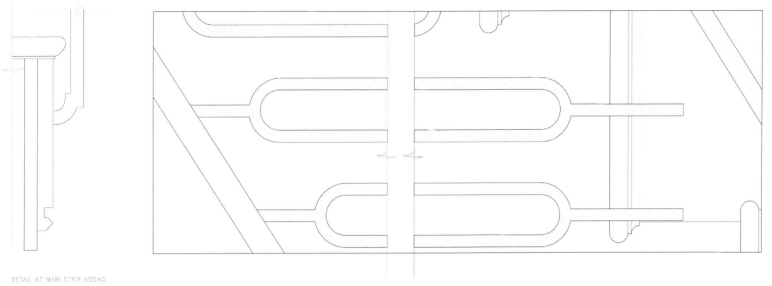

DETAIL AT MAIN STAIR NOSING

MAIN STAIR—STEEL BALUSTER DETAIL

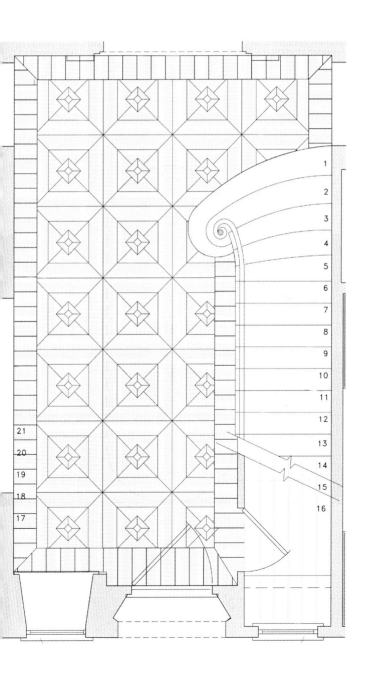

1
2
3
4
5
6
7
8
9
10
11
12
13
14
15
16

21
20
19
18
17

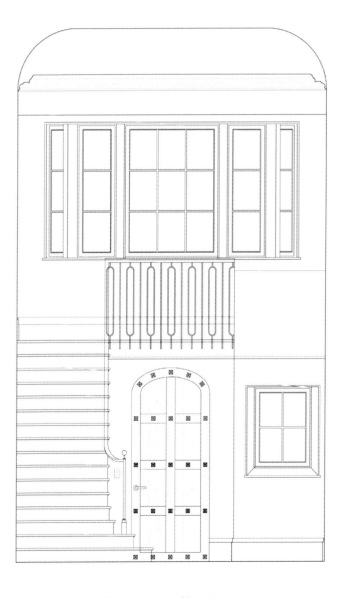

Elevation at Stair Hall

I magine that a wealthy American bought a classic farmhouse somewhere in the English countryside and then turned it into a modern retreat for himself and his young family. That idea served as the starting point for the stylistic inspiration of this house, which takes further cues from the work of the late, great American decorator Albert Hadley. I conceived the design to have a current yet established feel, mixing tradition with more contemporary furnishings and features—one of the many things at which Hadley excelled.

With these influences in its soul, this new home taps into an aesthetic—that of the "modern barn"—that's firmly rooted in the surrounding region's farming history and also happens to be enjoying a particular vogue these days. Just as the area's shingle style gave way in the 1960s to Cubist rectilinear houses by such modernists as Charles Gwathmey, there's now renewed interest in a style that takes the local vernacular of rustic agricultural buildings and makes from it something much more sophisticated.

Barns and farmhouses have a certain nostalgia about them, but, at the same time, their simplicity lends itself to a more modern look. The clean geometries and large openings are ideal for expansive windows and glass doors that let in light, and the ample space and open layouts of these building types allow for the kind of multifunctional rooms and flowing floor plans that twenty-first-century homeowners crave. This may take the form of a double-height living room, a large kitchen that gives on to a family room and dining area, or amply sized bedrooms—this house has seven—each with its own en-suite bathroom.

Rural England in particular proved fertile ground for ideas here because its farmhouses and other countryside homes wear their rustication beautifully on their sleeves, something appropriate for this relaxed family abode. Many of these English antecedents avoid ornamentation, instead deriving their visual interest and animation from intriguing textures, and the juxtaposition of smooth and rough. There's something of a naïve yet uncomplicated quality about these buildings, but they nonetheless have the ability to surprise, with powerful moments and grand architectural gestures unlike those seen anywhere else. I deployed these hallmarks in a variety of ways in this house.

Of particular note among the interiors' thoughtfully textured treatments are the dry, scraped-looking finishes, which become one of the home's most atmosphere-defining hallmarks. I wanted the place to seem like a centuries-old house, one that had recently been perfectly and lovingly restored. Walls are matte sand-texture plaster, coarse in some places, softer in others, a fact highlighted by the smooth, polished art and accents hung on and set against them. These

A staircase presents ample opportunity to introduce texture and drama into an entrance hall. This example features a modern iron balustrade capped by a wood railing, all set against curved plaster walls and parquet floors of antiqued scraped oak and marble.

Antiqued rafters, clerestory windows, and enormous steel-and-glass doors work together to add the texture, light, and scale and proportion that provide this enormous, clean-lined space with its rustic yet refined atmosphere. Relatively simple, modern furniture invites you to relax and put your feet up.

232

walls have an almost unfinished appearance that subtly suggests the feeling of a farmhouse. They also intrigue, making you wonder, "What is that material?" You want to reach out and touch it.

The floors offer a similar note, the rift-sawn white oak having been wire-brushed and scraped by hand to achieve a result that looks timeworn. They seem like the furthest thing from new, but, of course, that's exactly what they are. Though the finish of the floorboards is quite rusticated, they were installed in elevated ways: The kitchen, for example, shows off a diamond parquet, while the foyer has a square parquet set with cabochons of smooth marble.

The study offers a particularly profound portrait of dry, rubbed surfaces designed in refined ways. There, the matte material of the bolection mantelpiece—formed of cut stone rather than polished marble—has the patina of age about it. The white-oak paneling and built-in bookshelves, meanwhile, appear similarly untreated, though in fact they are washed over with glazes and diluted milk paints. I wanted the wood to look like it had been exposed to the elements for years, the passage of time lending it warmth. Even the rug, though new and made of soft New Zealand wool, looks as if it was woven from jute fibers and shows years of daily use. The details of the millwork read as relatively simple, but the chamfered edges and molding along the top rail take it to a level of ornament more elevated than what one would typically see in a common farmhouse.

With its clerestory window and barn-inspired rafters, the double-height living room presents a different but related interpretation of simplified woodwork and dry finishes. Its matte materials extend from the decoratively painted ceiling timbers to the French oak of the vintage sideboard opposite the sandblasted Portland cement mantel. The modern upholstered pieces—whose aesthetic channels Hadley and whose substantial scale and clean lines keep them in proportion with the rest of the room—provide contrasting softness and luxury, thanks to the rich textures of fine woven linen and loomed cotton.

Although secondary to the elements of style, texture, and scale and proportion in this house, light and color also work in concert here, and in important ways that lend a sense of atmosphere. The back of the large, open but private two-plus-acre property faces south, so the architect placed big-windowed entertaining and other vibrant public areas—living room, kitchen, family room—along the sun-flooded rear of the house. The more private spaces, like the library, as well as bathrooms and the main staircase, went along the darker, north-facing side.

Because the house enjoys an abundance of natural light in so many of its rooms, saturated colors would have appeared washed out. Instead, pale neutrals like flax, ivory, oatmeal, taupe, wheat,

In any season, a fireplace provides a focal point, helping center a space. This one boasts an antiqued custom mantel and surprisingly petite firebricks. The disc mirror above appears especially sculptural when set against the heavily textured, matte-finished sand-plaster wall.

Rhythm plays an important role here. Cutting against the room's symmetry, more than a dozen graphic black-and-white artworks are collaged in a balanced but syncopated geometric arrangement above a pair of lacquered consoles. **PAGE 238**: The works hung on the wall include those by Richard Giglio, Jean Cocteau, and Franz Kline. **PAGE 239**: Though disparate, a ceramic Chinese urn, marble Italian compote, metal Constantin Brâncuși–inspired gold sculpture, and porcelain Robert Kuo lamp share a simple sense of line and form.

and linen form a backdrop for occasional doses of slightly brighter hues, including sage, pistachio green, chocolate brown, and maize. The overall result has a warm, gentle glow, one that works well with the natural setting.

Despite the relative subtlety and restraint of the detailing, finishes, furnishings, and palette of this modern barn, the house is not without its wow moments—far from it, in fact. And these lend it a far-reaching feeling of atmosphere. The sense of scale in the living room is an example of one such feature. So, too, is the lofty, twenty-four-foot-high foyer. Its curving plaster walls, tea-paper ceiling, and elegantly forged balustrade give it a Continental attitude that blends classic and modern, just like the rest of the home.

Other moments in the house feel like site-specific installations: The width of the main upstairs hallway narrows toward one end, enveloping you as you proceed down it from the staircase to the bedrooms. Small niches set with small lanterns sit in its sand-plaster walls. The scheme borrows inspiration from Le Corbusier's iconic chapel at Ronchamp, France: the lamps' radiance warms the walls and illuminates the path as if the light were coming from votive candles.

In the dining room, I reimagined the different sized squares and rectangles of Versailles parquetry tiles to create a highly dimensional treatment on the walls. In this vertical installation,

Adjacent to both a large kitchen and the commodious living room, this sitting room has the relative intimacy of its scale to thank for its cozy atmosphere. Helping too are the sound-dampening padded walls, upholstered with a linen fabric.

THIS PAGE AND FOLLOWING PAGES: In the dining room, a feature wall made of beveled blocks of wood catches the light from a north-facing window. Its multidimensional shapes, as well as those of the simply carved, honed-marble mantel, give rise to intriguing shadows and highlights. Those hard surfaces are juxtaposed with chairs covered in nubby fabrics, ample wool curtains, soft wool challis shades, and a custom-made oversized Nepalese wool-and-silk rug. These materials keep the room just hushed enough, even during boisterous dinner parties.

the flooring becomes bisque-painted blocks that are puzzled together. The front of each is slightly angled, adding additional texture: The pieces fit snuggly, but their faces don't perfectly align to create a flat surface. The unique pattern provides texture, with shadows and highlights turning it into a bas-relief sculpture.

Elsewhere, the ceilings command attention. The segmented arch of the kitchen features the same Wedgewood-blue antique-glazed tiles that extend the height of the backsplash wall below; this draws the eye overhead, while also unifying the space, making it feel insulated and protective. For the master bedroom, I wanted something that had never been seen before, beyond a vault or timber treatment. Instead, I drew inspiration from the undulating curvature of a bell. That's not something taken directly from an English precedent—if anything, it owes more to Dutch architecture—but its purity of form remains true to the house's ethos and style.

These sensational design moments, like the house itself, are meant not just to be seen, but experienced as well. Beyond the specifics of the particular pieces of furniture or fabrics, the atmosphere of this house derives from a combination of intriguing, one-of-a-kind architectural statements and carefully considered and beautifully rendered dry finishes that create a rhythm throughout.

Designed for a family that loves to cook, the kitchen extracts maximum beauty from fairly simple details and combinations of fine materials used in novel ways: cerused-oak cabinets with insets of brushed stainless steel, a bronze-and-stainless-steel stove hood, an island of radius-edged breccia medicea marble, and antique glazed Wedgewood-blue tiles.

PREVIOUS PAGES: With its classical limestone bolection mantel and seventeenth-century Jacobean-style paneling in limed oak, the study feels masculine and scholarly. A mid-century wingback chair and contemporary side table finished with cracked-eggshell lacquer and brass trim serve as unexpected elements within this mise-en-scène. The room appears simultaneously ancient and modern, warm and sophisticated.
ABOVE AND OPPOSITE: Conceived to surprise and delight, the unique bell curve of the master suite's ceiling emphasizes the room's status as a singular space within the home. The smooth plaster finish of the walls and ceiling has a beautiful luster that helps reflect light from the windows as well as from the floor lamp, the Diego Giacometti–style white-plaster four-arm chandelier, and the Christopher Spitzmiller table lamp.

While the atmosphere of the master suite came largely from its ceiling, that of this guest room springs from the grand scale of its curtained canopy bed, which serves to anchor the space and to provide a focal point. Beyond the bed, an encaustic painting, colorful vintage glassware, a richly hued rug, and a shimmering lacquered ceiling also charm lucky guests.

ABOVE: The master bath exudes radiance and luster, from the shining marble floors to the polished white acrylic tub, and from the antiqued mirrored closet doors to the large windows only partially covered by sheer curtains. **OPPOSITE:** The architecturally detailed raftered ceiling in this guest bedroom helps create a sense of rhythm in the arrangement of furniture below, which includes a custom bed designed to fit perfectly between a pair of windows.

ABOVE: The Cubist-inspired bar in the basement enjoys brilliant light from an oversized window well. Architraves and other moldings were designed simply, edited to achieve a certain monastic style.
OPPOSITE: Winding down to the basement is a narrow, curving stair enclosed by the smoothest of plaster walls. A clerestory window bathes the steps in natural light even as they descend to a subterranean level.

Everything about the decor of the billiard room—which centers on a custom pool table made of cerused ebonized oak—is bold in scale, keeping it all in proportion to the room's ample overall size.

PART III

DETAILS COMPLETE
THE DESIGN

Whether you believe that it's God who's in the details or the Devil, the fact remains that the details matter if you want to create atmosphere. The architecture of a room comes first, of course, and many people, myself included, prefer to place any important art before getting to furnishings and other objects. But each component of a decorating scheme, no matter how small, must be thought of as it relates to the seven elements of great design—because everything has scale and proportion, color, texture.

Just as the style you select for a residence carries into the home's individual rooms, it must also extend to the selection of pieces within those spaces *and* their details. The rugs, for example, need you to make decisions about yarn type, luster, and pattern. No component is too small to escape notice, and every detail, therefore, demands insight and attention. A positive outcome requires the careful consideration of each part of a scheme, always with a definitive idea of how it will benefit the mood of an interior. This ensures that all the various components will appear unified and coherent, creating an atmosphere that delights and tantalizes the senses.

Details should be created and deployed within the context of the seven elements established in a space. In this study, most of the design features are of the classical order, and the room's relative simplicity stems largely from its nearly perfectly square shape. The moldings, for example, are slab style, while unfussy Doric columns serve as shelf supports. Providing contrast, the objects on the shelves are more freeform and organic. FOLLOWING PAGES: Taken together, details—like the elements themselves—can add up to much more than the sum of their parts. The quality and execution of each is important, but so, too, is authenticity and ingenuity. Details will enhance, refine, and serve as the "eye candy" of the overall design, the icing on the cake, and the essential finish to any successful space.

  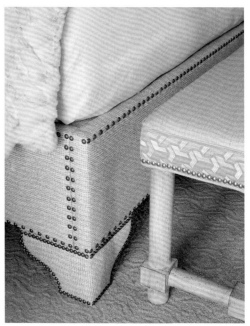

ABOVE: This space sits between a foyer with a bold, geometric black-and-white polished marble floor and a hallway with minimal treatment of its surfaces. To bridge the two areas, the drama here shifts from the floor to the walls, where a large-scaled abstract mural takes inspiration from the work of early-twentieth-century artist Fernand Léger and designer Le Corbusier. The details proceed from this period and their styles, as well as the shapes and colors of the painting. OPPOSITE: Details are the grace notes of the melody that is a room's atmosphere. Think of them as an opportunity to expand and elevate your use of the seven elements.

RESOURCES

ANTIQUE FURNITURE

1stdibs
www.1stdibs.com

A. Tyner Antiques
www.swedishantiques.biz

Brownrigg
www.brownrigg-interiors.co.uk

Guinevere
www.guinevere.co.uk

James Worrall
www.jamesworrall.com

John Rosselli Antiques
www.johnrosselliantiques.com

Kenny Ball Antiques
www.kennyballantiques.com

Lee Callicchio
www.leecalicchioltd.com

Lorfords
www.lorfordsantiques.com

Newel, LLC
www.newel.com

Parc Monceau
www.parcmonceauatl.com

Robuck
www.robuck.co

Sibyl Colefax & John Fowler
www.sibylcolefax.com

Spencer Swaffer antiques
www.spencerswaffer.com

ANTIQUE & REPRODUCTION MANTELS

A & R Asta Limited
www.astafireplaces.com

Chesney's
www.chesneys.com

Francois & Co.
www.francoisandco.com

Jamb Limited
www.jamb.co.uk.com

ART GALLERIES

Borghi Fine Art
www.borghifineart.com

Sears-Peyton Gallery
www.searspeyton.com

TEW Galleries
www.timothytew.com

CARPETS & RUGS

Eliko Rugs
www.elikorugs.com

Keivan Woven Arts
www.keivanwovenarts.com

NIBA Designs
www.nibadesigns.com

Stark Carpet
www.starkcarpet.com

DECORATIVE PAINTING

Bob Christian Decorative Art
www.bobchristiandecorativeart.com

Steven Floyd
www.stephenfloyddesign.com

DECORATIVE PLASTER & MOULDINGS

Balmer Architectural Mouldings
www.balmer.com

Hyde Park
631-752-7837

DOOR, WINDOW & CABINET HARDWARE

Frank Allart & Company
www.allart.co.uk

H. Theophile
www.htheophile.com

Katonah Architectural Hardware
www.katonahhardware.com

The Private World of Yves Saint Laurent & Pierre Bergé

PARISIAN INTERIORS

FABRICS

Ainsworth-Noah
www.ainsworth-noah.com

Chelsea Textiles – Editions
New York
www.chelseatextiles.com

Clarence House
www.clarencehouse.com

Cowtan & Tout
www.cowtan.com

Elitis
703-465-5512

Fortuny
www.fortuny.com

Grizzel & Mann
www.grizzelandmann.com

Holland & Sherry
www.hollandandsherry.com

Jasper
www.johnroselli.com

Jerry Pair
www.jerrypair.com

Kravet
www.kravet.com

Larsen
www.cowtan.com

Les Indiennes
www.lesindiennes.com

Manuel Canovas
www.manuelcanovas.com

Robert Kime
www.robertkime.com

Rogers & Goffigon
www.rogersandgoffigon.com

Romo
www.romo.com

Rose Tarlow Merlose House
www.rosetarlow.com

Samuel & Sons
www.samuelandsons.com

Schumacher
www.fschumacher.com

Travis & Company
www.travisandcompany.com

Tyler Graphics
202-319-1100

FURNITURE

Baker Furniture
www.bakerfurniture.com

David Iatesta
www.davidiatesta.com

Gustavo Olivieri
631-537-2811

Huntting House Antiques
www.hunttinghouseantiques.com

John Boone, Inc.
www.johnbooneinc.com

John Himmel Decorative Arts
www.johnhimmel.com

M. Southern Design Concepts
www.msoutherndesignconcepts.com

Mr. + Mrs. Howard for
Sherrill Furniture
www.sherrillfurniture.com

Mrs Howard
www.mrshoward.com

R Hughes
www.r-hughes.com

LIGHTING

Charles Edwards
www.charlesedwards.com

David Weeks Studio
www.davidweeksstudio.com

Jamb
www.jamb.co.uk

James Worrall
www.jamesworrall.com

Lorfords
www.lorfordsantiques.com

McLean Lighting Works
www.mcleanlighting.com

Paul Ferrante
www.paulferrante.com

The Urban Electric Co.
www.urbanelectricco.com

Vaughan
www.vaughandesign.com

Visual Comfort
www.visualcomfort.com

Waterworks
www.waterworks.com

PLUMBING FIXTURES,
FITTINGS & BATH
ACCESSORIES

Kohler
www.kohler.com

Lefroy Brooks
Usa.lefroybrooks.com

Watermark
www.watermark-designs.com

Waterworks
www.waterworks.com

STONE & TILE

Ann Sacks
www.annsacks.com

Exquisite Surfaces
www.xsurfaces.com

New Ravenna
www.newravenna.com

Paris Ceramics
www.parisceramics.com

Renaissance Tile
www.renaissancetileandbath.com

Waterworks
www.waterworks.com

WALLCOVERINGS

Cowtan & Tout
www.cowtan.com

Elizabeth Dow
www.elizabethdow.com

Galbraith & Paul
www.galbraithandpaul.com

Holland & Sherry
www.hollandandsherry.com

Phillip Jeffries
www.phillipjeffries.com

WORKROOMS

Highgrove Design
704-525-2130

M. Southern Design Concepts
www.msoutherndesignconcepts.com

Willard Pitt Curtain Makers
404-355-8232

ACKNOWLEDGMENTS

Discovering the inspiration that allows me to find unique design solutions is definitely not easy, but it is the essential ingredient in making homeowners' dreams reality. Luckily, I find daily inspiration in the people whose houses I have the great pleasure of decorating. They are the most important aspect of any project, as nothing happens without them, and so I must begin by thanking them for their support and patience over the years. Their encouragement, guidance, and friendship have been some of the most important forces in my life.

From there, I can only try to adequately acknowledge all those who have contributed to the making of this book—including everyone from God above to decorative painters Bob Christian and Stephen Floyd, whose work adorns many a wall, floor, and ceiling in the houses I've designed. And then there are all the draftsmen and project managers from my studio who turn ideas and thumbnail sketches into the beautiful drawings and renderings that become wonderful houses. Their work, along with that of the passionate architects with whom I've been privileged to collaborate—including William T. Baker, Peter Block, D. Stanley Dixon, Bobby McAlpine, and Greg Tankersley—make my job a joy.

Thanks to the brilliance, talent, and vision of photographers Lucas Allen, Max Kim-Bee, Miguel Flores-Vianna, Emily Followill, and Eric Piasecki, as well as stylists Carolyn Englefield and Leslie Newsome Rascoe, the interiors I design look their absolute best. Shawna Mullen, and the rest of the team at Abrams, including managing editor Annalea Manalili, design manager Danny Maloney, and assistant editor Hayley Salmon, had the vision to bring my work to life in this volume, and, for that, I'll be forever grateful. And I have nothing but praise and appreciation for book designer Doug Turshen and his associate David Huang; they took a box of photographs and artfully arranged them into a book that I am extremely proud of. Doug also led me to writer and editor Andrew Sessa, whose intelligence, keen ear, and insight helped me craft the explanations of my design process and the descriptions of the houses in these pages.

My mom and dad were wonderful parents who taught me common sense and the importance of working hard, of honesty, and of just plain showing up. I hope they were proud of me for what I have done to fulfill my dreams. They taught me how to be a father to my own children, Max, Ashley, Nellie, and Andrew—the last two of whom work with me, and continually remind me that their own future decorating books will be much better than mine.

Finally, I must share my undying appreciation for my wife, Phoebe, the famous Mrs. Howard, who first urged me to write this book and guided me through every step. She has been a perpetual source of love, reassurance, and fortitude through all the late nights and weekends, poring over the layouts and manuscripts, offering sound guidance and an unerring eye. Phoebe never distracted me—except to ask me to go to the grocery store, or to pour her a drink, or to find her iPad, or, of course, to point out that she is the better author. And I'll love her forever for all of it. Thank you, Phoebe. I hope that someday, one of our many grandchildren will pick up this book and be drawn into this wonderful profession we share, saying, "I want to be just like them."

PHOTO CREDITS

Lucas Allen: pages 28, 30, 31, 47, 63, 71, 74, 75, 85, 200–227, 230–261, 262 (images 2/4/9), 263 (images 1/7/8), 265 (images 4/5)

Erica George Dines: 61

Miguel Flores-Vianna: 21, 35, 67, 68, 77, 270

Josh Gibson: 22, 39, 265 (images 7/9)

Tria Giovan: 14, 262 (image 5), 265 (image 2)

Nick Johnson: 42

Max Kim-Bee: 2, 3, 4, 5, 16, 19, 25, 27, 32, 45, 46, 51, 54, 55, 56, 72, 79, 82, 86, 88–121, 156–197, 262 (images 3/6/7), 263 (images 4/5/6/9), 265 (images 1/3/6/8)

Francesco Lagnese: 8, 9

Nancy Nolan: 59

Eric Piasecki: 6, 7, 10, 11, 40, 52, 65, 66, 81, 122–153, 262 (images 1/8), 263 (images 2/3), 264

Alan Shortall: 24, 49

Editor: Shawna Mullen
Designer: Doug Turshen with David Huang
Production Manager: Rebecca Westall

Library of Congress Control Number: 2018936274

ISBN: 978-1-4197-3076-4
eISBN: 978-1-68335-512-0

Printed and bound in China
10 9 8 7 6 5 4 3 2

Abrams books are available at special discounts when purchased in quantity
for premiums and promotions as well as fundraising or educational use. Special
editions can also be created to specification. For details, contact specialsales@
abramsbooks.com or the address below.

Abrams® is a registered trademark of Harry N. Abrams, Inc.

ABRAMS The Art of Books
195 Broadway, New York, NY 10007
abramsbooks.com